Study Skills for **Linguistics**

Study Skills for Linguistics is the essential companion for students embarking on a degree in linguistics. Covering all the core skills that students of linguistics will require during the early part of their degree, this book gives the reader a basic understanding of the field, as well as confidence in how to find out more and how to prepare for their future career.

The key features covered include:

- subject-specific skills including basic linguistic tools and terminology, such as word classes and grammatical terminology;
- essential study skills, such as how to perform well in the degree, how to search for and reference literature and how to write an essay;
- guides for a future with a linguistics degree, including how to write a CV and prepare for a range of graduate destinations.

An accessible guide to essential skills in the field of linguistics, *Study Skills for Linguistics* is a must-read for students contemplating studying this topic, and provides a guide that will take them through their degree and beyond.

Jeanette Sakel is Senior Lecturer in Linguistics at the University of the West of England. Her main research interests include language contact, bilingualism, linguistic typology, fieldwork, native South American languages, bilingual education, and supplementary schools.

D0162061

Understanding Language series

Series Editors:

Bernard Comrie, Max Planck Institute for Evolutionary Anthropology, Leipzig, Germany
Greville Corbett, Surrey Morphology Group, University of Surrey, UK

The Understanding Language series provides approachable, yet authoritative, introductions to major topics in linguistics. Ideal for students with little or no prior knowledge of linguistics, each book carefully explains the basics, emphasizing understanding of the essential notions rather than arguing for a particular theoretical position.

Other titles in the series:

Understanding Pragmatics
Gunter Senft

Understanding Child Language Acquisition
Caroline Rowland

Understanding Semantics, Second Edition
Sebastian Löbner

Understanding Syntax, Fourth Edition
Maggie Tallerman

Understanding Phonetics
Patricia Ashby

Understanding Phonology, Third Edition
Carlos Gussenhoven
Haike Jacobs

Understanding Morphology, Second Edition
Martin Haspelmath
Andrea D. Sims

Understanding Language Testing
Dan Douglas

Understanding Second Language Acquisition
Lourdes Ortega

For more information on any of these titles, or to order, go to
www.routledge.com/linguistics

Study Skills for
Linguistics

Jeanette Sakel

Routledge
Taylor & Francis Group

LONDON AND NEW YORK

First published 2015
by Routledge
2 Park Square, Milton Park, Abingdon, Oxon OX14 4RN

and by Routledge
711 Third Avenue, New York, NY 10017

Routledge is an imprint of the Taylor & Francis Group, an informa business

© 2015 Jeanette Sakel

British Library Cataloguing in Publication Data
A catalogue record for this book is available from the British Library

Library of Congress Cataloging in Publication Data
Sakel, Jeanette, 1973-
Study skills for linguistics / Jeanette Sakel.
pages cm. -- (Understanding language series)
Includes bibliographical references and index.
1. Linguistics. 2. Linguistics--Study and teaching (Higher) 3. Linguistic analysis (Linguistics) I. Title.
P126.S23 2015
418.0071--dc23
2014039264

ISBN: 978-0-415-72045-8 (hbk)
ISBN: 978-0-415-72046-5 (pbk)
ISBN: 978-1-315-72415-7 (ebk)

Typeset in Minion Pro
by Saxon Graphics Ltd, Derby

Printed and bound in the United States of America by Publishers Graphics, LLC on sustainably sourced paper.

Contents

List of figures   viii
List of tables   ix
Preface   x
Acknowledgements   xi
List of abbreviations   xiii

1 Introduction   **1**
1.1 Studying linguistics   1
1.2 Three subfields of linguistics   2
1.3 Skills   3
1.4 Introduction to each of the chapters   4
1.5 The format of the book   4
1.6 Self-reflection and awareness of skills   5

2 What is language?   **10**
2.1 Defining language   10
2.2 Spoken and written language   11
2.3 Sign languages   14
2.4 Other ways of expressing language   16
2.5 Spoken and endangered languages   17
2.6 The number of languages in the world   17
2.7 Writing down spoken languages   18
2.8 Prescriptive versus descriptive approaches to language   20
2.9 Summary: how to define *language*?   20

3 Sounds   **23**
3.1 Spoken language   23
3.2 Vowels   25
3.3 Consonants   27
3.4 Other types of pronunciation   30
3.5 The study of sounds   30

4 Word classes   **33**
4.1 Words   33
4.2 Dictionaries   34
4.3 Dividing words into classes   35

4.4	Nouns	36
4.5	Verbs	38
4.6	Adjectives	41
4.7	Adverbs	41
4.8	Pronouns	42
4.9	Particles and other word classes	42
4.10	A word of caution	43
4.11	Word classes in the languages of the world	43

5   The grammar of words — **46**

5.1	Morphemes	46
5.2	Different types of morphemes	47
5.3	Derivation	49
5.4	Inflection	49
5.5	Agreement in the clause	57

6   Clauses and sentences — **61**

6.1	Word order	61
6.2	Phrases	63
6.3	Subjects and objects	64
6.4	Semantic roles	65
6.5	Predicates	65
6.6	Other syntactic concepts: questions, negation, voice	66
6.7	Complex sentences: coordination and subordination	68

7   Meaning and discourse — **71**

7.1	Lexical meaning	71
7.2	Synonymy, antonymy, hyponymy	73
7.3	The logic of language: inference, proposition and presupposition	73
7.4	Meaning and context: pragmatics	74
7.5	Texts: coherence and cohesion	75
7.6	The analysis of discourse	76

8   Understanding approaches to language: theory and practice — **78**

8.1	Reports on research	78
8.2	Theories, hypotheses and gaining new insights	79
8.3	Empirical and theoretical approaches	80
8.4	Theoretical linguistics	81
8.5	Descriptive linguistics	81
8.6	Language change and prescriptive grammar	82
8.7	Critical thinking and evaluation of research	83

9   Research methods: collecting, analysing and presenting data — **85**

9.1	Finding a research question	85
9.2	Data	86

9.3   Methods for different problems   87
9.4   Different types of data collection   90
9.5   Operationalization   94
9.6   Working with data   94
9.7   Research ethics   96
9.8   Presentation of results and alternative analyses   97

10 Assessment: presenting your skills   99
10.1 Working independently   99
10.2 Writing an essay or report   100
10.3 Giving presentations   105
10.4 Performing well in exams   106
10.5 Summary: how to achieve good marks   107

11 How to find out more about language   109
11.1 Researching a topic   109
11.2 Terminology   110
11.3 Types of academic publications   110
11.4 How to use the information you find   112
11.5 Understanding difficult texts   113
11.6 Libraries and other resources at your university   114
11.7 How to expand your range of expertise   114

12 Careers: what to do with linguistics and how to get a job 117
12.1 Typical careers of linguistics graduates   117
12.2 Generic skills for careers   118
12.3 Skills and preparation for specific careers   120
12.4 Preparing for life after graduation   124
12.5 Writing a CV   124
12.6 Preparing for a job interview   125

13 Personal development   127
13.1 Reflecting on your own language use   127
13.2 Evaluating and challenging attitudes   128
13.3 Style   129
13.4 English among the languages of the world   130
13.5 Practical outcomes   130
13.6 The big question: when will I know it all?   131

References   132
Glossary   135
Index of languages   159
Index   160

Figures

3.1	IPA, vowels	26
3.2	Places of articulation	28
3.3	IPA, consonants	29
10.1	Typical sections of an essay	102
12.1	Typical careers for linguistics graduates	118

Tables

5.1	English personal pronouns	51
5.2	The English verbal paradigm	57
5.3	The Spanish verbal paradigm	58
10.1	The essay-writing process	100

Preface

Since you picked up this book on *study skills for linguistics*, you are probably studying (or at least considering studying) linguistics. There is a wide range of reasons for people to choose to study linguistics: some students develop an interest in language at school, some choose linguistics for the breadth of the field and the wide range of employment options, others have an interest in learning new languages and want to know more about how to approach this successfully. This may apply to you, or you may have other motivations. Whatever your reasons, linguistics can be a really rewarding subject to study. This book is aimed at all of you and is structured in such a way that you can select individual chapters that are most relevant to you, yet you can also read the book cover to cover if you prefer.

My aim is to prepare you for a university course in linguistics and to give you the confidence to know how to progress and do well on a course in linguistics. Even more ambitiously, I hope that this book will serve as a companion throughout your degree, a book you will pick up again from time to time as you reach different milestones, such as your first exam, writing an essay, conducting your 'own' empirical study and writing job applications.

Acknowledgements

This book came about after Greville Corbett's suggestion to write something aimed at incoming students, introducing basic linguistic terminology and skills such as how to write essays and approach time management. I was very enthusiastic about this idea, feeling that a book of this kind would be really useful to recommend to incoming students or those in the first year of their course. This resulted in many exchanges with the series editors Bernard Comrie and Greville Corbett, whose insightful comments helped me enormously during the entire process, from the proposal to the final product. I am also indebted to Penny Everson for her comments on the final draft of the manuscript.

I am very grateful for the time and energy the team at Taylor & Francis have put into working with me, in particular Rachel Daw, Nigel Hope, Nadia Seemungal and Helen Tredget. I also highly appreciate the input from Lucy Rowland, with whom I worked on the initial book proposal.

Yet, the most important input to this book came from my students: their questions and comments have greatly shaped the way this book is laid out. Space prevents me from mentioning them all, but I want to express particular thanks to the following students and graduates: Victoria Adcock, Maryam Bham, Joshua Creaven, Emily Duignan, Zoe Egan, Dave Etheridge, Craig Evans, Rosie Fletcher, Alice Goodwin, Amy Haines, Joanna Jackson, Antonia Kelly, Gina Ko, Chris Loughlin, Victoria Mercer, Gemma May Osborne, Chaweewan Puntun, Sandy Sond, Lisa Stevens, Matt Vicker, Tom Warner, Taylor Wearne and Tanya Woll.

My colleagues at the University of the West of England also served as inspiration, and took part in many a discussion about study skills, employability and linguistic terminology. Particular regards go to my Programme team, in particular Kate Beeching, Jonathan Charteris-Black, Richard Coates, Rebecca Fong, Petros Karatsareas, James Murphy, Anna Piasecki and Catherine Rosenberg.

My warmest thanks go to a number of people who inspired me, either with their approach to teaching or with their support during the writing process: Ellen Berchner-Nolan, Michael Daller, Eva Eppler, Dan Everett, Isabella Griffiths, Dick Hudson, Jeanine Treffers-Daller and Viveka Velupillai. I would not have been able to write this book without the immense support from my lovely family: Patrick and Maya.

Thanks to mobile technology, I was lucky to be able to write parts of this book in an area of ancient woodland, the Lower Woods, among wildflowers and butterflies.

The author and publishers would like to thank the following copyright holders for permission to reproduce the following material:

IPA Chart, http://www.langsci.ucl.ac.uk/ipa/ipachart.html, available under a Creative Commons Attribution-Sharealike 3.0 Unported License. Copyright © 2005 International Phonetic Association.

Illustration of the places of articulation © Patrick Thornhill, reproduced with kind permission.

Front page photo © Jeanette Sakel, *Epipactis Helleborine var. Albiflora*, South Gloucestershire 2014.

Abbreviations

1 or 1st	first person ('I' or 'we')
2 or 2nd	second person ('you')
3 or 3rd	third person ('he', 'she', 'it', 'they')
ABL	ablative case, a way to mark nouns in some languages
ABS	absolutive case, a way to mark nouns in some languages
ALL	allative case, a way to mark nouns in some languages
C	consonant (in the context of syllable structure)
CELTA	Certificate in Teaching English to Speakers of other Languages
CV	curriculum vitae
ELAN	a program designed for transcribing language
F	feminine gender
IND	indicative mood, a way to mark verbs in some languages
INF	infinitive
IPA	the International Phonetic Alphabet
M	masculine gender
MA	Master of Arts, a postgraduate qualification
NEG	negation marker
O	object (in the context of word order)
OBJ	object (in a gloss)
OED	*The Oxford English Dictionary*
OSV	object–subject–verb word order
OVS	object–verb–subject word order
PAL	peer-assisted learning
PASS	passive voice

PGCE	postgraduate certificate in education
PhD	Doctor of Philosophy, a postgraduate qualification
PL	plural number
PRF	perfect aspect
S	subject (in the context of word order)
SG	singular number
SUBJ	subject (in a gloss)
SVO	subject–verb–object word order
TED	TED ('technology, entertainment, design') talk online
TESOL	Teachers of English to Speakers of Other Languages
UCAS	the Universities and Colleges Admissions Service
V	verb (in the context of word order)
V	vowel (in the context of syllable structure)
wh	interrogative pronoun (word of the type *what, when, who*)
X	placeholder for an element different from Y and Z
Y	placeholder for an element different from X and Z
Z	placeholder for an element different from X and Y

Introduction

IN THIS CHAPTER

This first chapter sets out to explain what the study of linguistics is about. I will be looking at a number of areas of linguistics, and then move on to the skills you will be developing during your studies, outlining how the book is laid out. In particular, this chapter includes:

- An introduction to the field of linguistics

- Examples from sociolinguistics, psycholinguistics and language typology

- An introduction to different kinds of skills developed in this book

- An overview of the book

- A number of exercises that look at your development as a student of linguistics.

1.1 STUDYING LINGUISTICS

Linguistics is the study of language from a wide range of different perspectives. It encompasses many different subdisciplines, some of which may be familiar to you, for example areas we could label as *grammar, children's language acquisition* and *differences in language use by old and young speakers*. These disciplines are often studied as part of the 'English Language' curriculum at school. Yet, there are many other ways to study language. Some of these are explored in the next section below.

While linguistics is a discipline in its own right, it also overlaps with other fields such as sociology, anthropology, philosophy, literature, psychology and computer sciences, and furthermore informs the related fields of language learning and teaching. Studying French, German, Chinese or even English Language, it is likely that you will come into contact with linguistics.

Some of the subareas of linguistics are *language acquisition, grammar,* the links between culture and language (*anthropological linguistics*), how we understand and produce language (*psycholinguistics*), the differences and similarities between the languages of the world (*linguistic typology*), the study of sound (*phonetics* and *phonology*), the study of different theories of grammar beyond the basic grammar learnt at school (a wide range of theories in *morphology* and *syntax*, for example *Role and Reference Grammar* and *Lexical Functional Grammar*), the study of meaning (*semantics* and *pragmatics*), the study of historical *language change*, as well as language change arising from *multilingualism* and *language contact*.

Linguistics is sometimes divided up into *theoretical linguistics* and *applied linguistics*, yet the two overlap in many ways. Most areas mentioned above would qualify as theoretical linguistics. Applied linguistics, as the name implies, aims to relate to real-world applications of the field. It includes disciplines such as *second language acquisition* and *language teaching*, the analysis of spoken and written *discourse*, language in its social setting (*sociolinguistics*), the study of multilingualism, *forensic linguistics* and more. The division between such 'applied' and 'theoretical' approaches is not necessarily clear-cut, as many traditionally 'theoretical' subjects have real-world applications as well. For example, studies on the way the brain stores and processes language can inform the way in which surgical procedures on the brain are conducted.[1]

1.2 THREE SUBFIELDS OF LINGUISTICS

Before we get started with skills and terminology, I want to give you examples from three areas of linguistics. These are sociolinguistics, psycholinguistics and language typology.

Sociolinguistics is an area of study that looks at language use in different social settings. Sometimes people speak different *dialects*. Yet, not all people from the same area use dialectal features in quite the same way. You may feel that people from rural settings have more pronounced dialects. Also, people of a working-class background may speak with a stronger accent than those of a middle-class background. Even speakers of different ages vary in their language use. Young people may use slang that other generations do not understand, while older people may use *words* that young native speakers of the same language would not actively use. All of this, and more, is studied by sociolinguists, who aim to explain variation within the language use of individuals and society. Sociolinguistics helps us to understand, for example, how different dialects form and how language changes over time.

Psycholinguistics, as the name implies, deals with the psychological dimensions of language. For example, psycholinguists study how language is produced and perceived, that is how speakers form utterances in their mind and understand utterances that others make. It is not always possible to look into speakers' brains to see how language works, even though advances in technology have started to make this possible, which is studied in the related field of neurolinguistics. In order to understand how speakers process language in their brain, psycholinguists set up specific experiments. Looking at the time it takes a speaker to recognize a word written on the screen, for example, can give them insights into the way the brain works. Some words may take longer for a speaker to recognize than others, which can lead to conclusions about word processing in the brain.

Linguistic typology is an area of linguistics that takes into account all languages of the world and classifies these according to their features (such as their sounds and grammar). Comparing the *structures* of the languages of the world, we can see that most languages use elements such as *nouns* and *verbs*, yet there are languages that do not make a clear distinction between the two. Also, many languages have so-called *complex sentence* structures (see chapter 6), but there are a handful of languages where that is not the case. Studying typology, we can learn what is common and what is special about languages. We can see that a number of features of English are highly uncommon *cross-linguistically*. Sometimes languages are similar because they have arisen from the same source and are related. The Romance languages in Europe are such an example. They include French, Spanish, Portuguese, Italian, Romanian and a number of smaller languages, and have all arisen from Latin. In other cases, languages resemble each other through language contact because they are spoken by the same bilingual speakers, not because the languages are related. We refer to this as language contact. In other cases, languages are similar because of the universal way in which speakers think, or organize their communication. Typology can help us find structures that are typical or common forms of language, shedding light on the way humans organize their communication. All three areas of linguistics discussed here ultimately tell us more about human nature.

In order to learn more about these or other areas of linguistics, it is necessary to have a solid understanding of the sound systems of languages, grammar and meaning. This will help you to capture the diverse ways in which language can be used, for example in different social settings, across the languages of the world or through language processing in the brain. These basic skills usually form part of a linguistics degree, and are often topics you have to learn more about before progressing on to other subareas of linguistics. To help you on the way, I discuss the basic terminology regarding sounds, grammar and meaning in chapters 3–7 below.

When it comes to the other fields of linguistics taught on a degree course, universities vary a lot. You will probably get an introduction to the fields mentioned above, but what exactly you are taught depends on the theoretical outlook and expertise at your university. In the UK, *subject benchmark statements* give an indication of the subfields typically taught on a degree course in linguistics (see further reading below).

Whether you are studying a course that is highly practical and applied or one that is theoretical and focuses on specific aspects of linguistics, the present book aims to help you get started and to get the best out of your university experience. Rather than introducing all that linguistics is about, the aim of this book is to equip you with the most basic skills to get the most out of your studies. Once you have mastered these, you will be well prepared to explore how language works in further detail.

1.3 SKILLS

University study often starts at a basic level and becomes quite complicated in due course. Yet, even at the beginning, your lecturers may expect you to know some terminology, such as noun, *preposition* and *clause*. Sometimes, students come with very different knowledge. Those who have studied other languages may be highly familiar with these concepts. Others may have had little input on language at school. I will discuss some of the basic language and linguistics terminology in chapters 3–7. Knowing the subject-specific terminology will give you confidence in dealing with any more complex approaches to language you encounter at a later stage.

Likewise, universities tend to expect you to know how to approach your studies, for example how to write an essay, find literature in the library or learn about a new topic of study. Understanding and being able to use these study skills can help you do well, gaining a good degree classification, find internships during your studies and employment upon graduation. A wide variety of study skills are discussed in the latter half of this book. These skills can sometimes also be applied in entirely unrelated situations. For example, knowing how to give a presentation is important during your course, but may come in useful in other situations, such as giving a speech at a wedding or being interviewed for a job. Skills that can be transferred to other areas than the narrow subject you are studying are generally referred to as *transferable skills*. They include essay-writing, knowing how to do well in exams, knowing how to find employment after graduation and finding out further information about specific topics.

Finally, there are *personal skills* and personal development, which are intrinsically linked to studying for a degree, yet may not always be easy to grasp. You may not be aware of it yourself until you reflect back, but you are likely to change your attitudes, behaviours or general outlook on life during a degree. I will briefly look at personal skills relating to a linguistics degree at the end of the book.

1.4 INTRODUCTION TO EACH OF THE CHAPTERS

This book introduces you to study skills that will help you succeed in a linguistics degree. The first part of the book looks at terminology and subject-specific skills in linguistics. In chapter 2, I will gradually work towards a definition of 'language'. Chapter 3 is a brief introduction to the sounds of language, also referred to as phonetics and phonology. Word classes are discussed in chapter 4, while chapter 5 goes into some detail with morphology and the grammar affecting words of different word classes. The following chapter 6 is about sentences, also called syntax. Chapter 7 goes into detail with meaning, in particular semantics and pragmatics. Chapter 8 introduces theories, hypotheses and research practice, and goes into detail with critical reflection on statements about language. Chapter 9 introduces a few methods that you can use in carrying out your own research on language. Chapter 10 is all about assessment, and discusses ways in which you can do well in exams, coursework and presentations. In chapter 11, I have collected a number of tips on how to find out more about language. Chapter 12 answers the question of what you can do with a linguistics degree, giving you a number of ideas and pointers for how to prepare for different types of careers. Finally, chapter 13 looks at your personal development from studying linguistics.

1.5 THE FORMAT OF THE BOOK

The chapters in this book begin with a short bullet-point summary of the contents, highlighting the main points of the text. Each chapter contains a number of exercises, which usually appear throughout the text, and in some cases at the end of a chapter. Some of these exercises are exploratory and do not lead to definite answers. In other cases, I provide an answer embedded in the text following the exercise.

If you want to know more about a topic, the section to look out for is 'further reading', which appears after the main text in each chapter. I recommend books and resources that you may find useful if you want to read more about the subject. To keep this book easily readable, I only give a minimum of *references* to other literature within the main text. These are usually sources for data or other books I quote.

The terminology in this book is based on the basic terminology used in the field of linguistics, in coordination with a glossary of 'grammatical terminology for schools', developed by the Education Committee of the Linguistics Association of Great Britain, led by Dick Hudson (2014: http://www.lagb-education.org/grammatical-terminology-for-schools). New terms that are presented in the glossary at the end of the book are *highlighted* in the text (appearing in italics and underlined) at their first occurrence. Elements in *italics* that are not underlined are, by common convention, examples of language data.

1.6 SELF-REFLECTION AND AWARENESS OF SKILLS

As you study linguistics, you may feel that some approaches are more interesting than others. Certain skills may be useful, while others appear less so. There are two extremes at which you can approach your studies: follow your interests, disregarding the less relevant things; or follow a clear career trajectory, focusing on skills that help you reach a specific goal.

During my own undergraduate and graduate studies, I was mainly doing the former, following my interests much more than any career-specific goal. I have found that this approach paid dividends. Sometimes, much later, a skill I never thought would come in useful turned out to make the difference between, for example, receiving funding for further study or not. If you are truly interested in something, you will be more motivated and more likely to do well.

Yet, it is highly advisable to have some awareness of possible careers early on in your studies. Exclusively following your interests, without aiming for specific goals could mean that you are missing out on valuable opportunities. You do not have to have a career in mind in order to target your acquisition of skills. Many skills are useful in different areas, and having a wide skill-set can open up new opportunities at a later stage. It is a good idea to combine a little bit of both the interest and the career goals. If you can bundle your interests and resources in such a way that you can gain a wide range of skills during your studies, you will stand a good chance to find employment and to have a choice in the types of careers you could explore upon graduation.

The exercises below target your current skills level, and can be used as a guideline throughout your career for developing skills.

Exercise 1.1

Who I am, and what I want to get out of this book:

It is a good idea to reflect on your own skills, before embarking on the remainder of this book. Try to jot down, in any order:

a   Why did you pick up this book?

b   What do you want to get out of studying linguistics (and/or language subjects)?

c   Which skills do you have?

d   Which skills would you like to develop?

e   What type of job would you like to do once you have studied linguistics (and/or language subjects)?

Exercise 1.2

The personal development record

At all times throughout your degree, it is a good idea to take stock, to understand where you are in your learning journey. Having this understanding will help you develop in areas you feel are important for yourself or that are essential for certain careers. Having done exercise 1 above, you can now think about how you can develop your skills during your study of linguistics. Try to be honest in your self-assessment:

My confidence in writing (e.g. writing an essay)

Where I am now: _____

What I want to achieve: _____

My confidence in speaking (giving a presentation)

Where I am now: _____

What I want to achieve: _____

Time management (working independently)

Where I am now: _____

What I want to achieve: _____

Reading (being able to read and understand academic literature)

Where I am now: _____

What I want to achieve: _____

Terminology (e.g. knowing what *prepositions* are)

Where I am now: _____

What I want to achieve: _____

Doing well during university study (knowing how to achieve a good degree classification)

Where I am now: _____

What I want to achieve: _____

IT skills (e.g. using word processing, setting up a blog, using specialized programs to analyse sound)

Where I am now: _____

What I want to achieve: _____

Do your own research (e.g. collecting data from speakers)

Where I am now: _____

What I want to achieve: _____

The future (preparing for being able to get a job after your degree, presenting yourself and your skills)

Where I am now: _____

What I want to achieve: _____

Critically evaluating others' research (e.g. understanding and evaluating the newest findings regarding language discussed in newspapers)

Where I am now: _____

What I want to achieve: _____

Working in teams

Where I am now: _____

What I want to achieve: _____

Showing initiative

Where I am now: _____

What I want to achieve: _____

Knowing where to find out more information (library, online resources; how to expand your range of knowledge with the wealth of information available)

Where I am now: _____

What I want to achieve: _____

Networking skills (e.g. LinkedIn)

Where I am now: _____

What I want to achieve: _____

Being able to reflect on own or others' language use (e.g. social aspirations, speech errors)

Where I am now: _____

What I want to achieve: _____

Changing attitudes (e.g. towards low status varieties, spelling: does it matter?)

Where I am now: _____

What I want to achieve: _____

Using the tools to learn new languages, writing in appropriate style, communicating efficiently

Where I am now: _____

What I want to achieve: _____

It is a good idea to keep this record, and to re-evaluate your progress throughout your degree. If you have a personal tutor or mentor, it could also be a good idea to discuss the list with them, in order to keep track of your own development.

FURTHER READING

If you want to know more about the study of language in general, and linguistics in particular, there are a number of good introductory books that will give you an overview of the field.

For example, Yule (2014) *The study of language*, now in its fifth edition, is a good and highly accessible introduction to language and linguistics, introducing the different fields of analysis (sounds, grammar, meaning), as well as a wide range of areas of language study (psycholinguistics, first language acquisition and so on). There are also chapters about language development, sign languages, and the intersections of language and culture.

Another, detailed introduction to linguistics is McGregor's (2009) *Introduction to linguistics*.

There are not many other books that target study skills in linguistics at this early stage. Most study-skills books are aimed at students during later stages in their degree, e.g. for conducting research studies (cf. Wray & Bloomer 2012; Sealey 2010). Other books look in more detail at literature and language, such as Pope (2012).

If you are interested in the topics typically taught as part of a linguistics degree, as well as the skills that are typically developed as part of this degree, the UK benchmark statements for linguistics may be interesting for you to look at. Since web-links change, I give you the most appropriate terms, presented 'in inverted commas' to put into a search engine (such as *Google*), which will help you to find the relevant literature. In this case, try to search for 'linguistics benchmark statement'.

NOTE

1 In recent years, researchers in all areas have been encouraged to make their studies applicable to the 'real world', showing that they can impact on the knowledge, behaviour or actions of others.

What is language?

IN THIS CHAPTER

This chapter discusses what makes up language, attempting a definition of the phenomenon of language. I will also discuss different ways in which communication can take place. In particular, I will look at:

- Definitions of language

- Spoken and written language

- Sign language, including baby signing

- Indigenous languages

- Descriptive and prescriptive approaches to language.

2.1 DEFINING LANGUAGE

What is language? Why, that is an easy question, surely? Or is it? I reckon if we wanted to find a definition for language, we would say that language is spoken, that people use it to communicate. Yet, someone may counter, language can also be written. Furthermore, in the case of *sign languages*, languages can be signed. Language can also exist merely as thought, and even then used as a medium for communication, for example in thought-controlled devices for severely disabled people. In this case it is neither spoken, written, nor signed. If we wanted to define all that is language, we would have to capture these different channels of communication in our definition. We could, for example, say that language is visible, audible or perceptible in other ways.

Despite the differences between the channels of language, they all transmit information and facilitate communication. Yet, the way in which meaning is transmitted is not necessarily straightforward. For example, the words or signs used to represent the thing talked about often have very little to do with that thing itself. Take, for example, the English word *dog*. There is no real link between this word and the animal itself. Other languages use different words to refer to the same animal, e.g. *hund* (Danish), *koira* (Finnish), *perro* (Spanish), *achae* (Mosetén). Hence, the relationship between the animal 'dog' and the word used for it is random, conventional and *arbitrary*. We have to learn the word in order to know that a speaker refers to a dog, as there is nothing in the word itself that gives away this information.

Well, you could say why not refer to our dog as a *woof.* This is an *onomatopoeic* expression, modelled on the sounds a dog makes. In this way, there is a relationship between the linguistic expression and the real world. However, most words in a language are not onomatopoeic. Furthermore, even onomatopoeia can be quite different across languages, and thus partially arbitrary. For example, a German dog utters *wauwau*, in Finnish it is *hau* and in Mosetén *wäshken*. Yet, the phenomenon of onomatopoeia is possible evidence of how language first developed. There are various approaches to this question, in particular to establish how human language can be distinguished from animal communication. This issue has been debated at great length, and I will return to it briefly in chapter 8. For now, let us look at what makes up (human) language as it is.

2.2 SPOKEN AND WRITTEN LANGUAGE

First of all, let us have a look in more detail at the different channels of language. Spoken language, for example, can take very different forms, depending on the situation in which it is used: a student giving a well-prepared presentation in class, three friends in a bar planning a trip abroad, a woman presenting her latest poem at a formal reading, a mother talking quietly to her baby and a professor answering her students' questions in a seminar.

In all of these situations, spoken language is used slightly differently. A well-prepared presentation is typically more *formal* than a chat about the next holiday among friends. The presentation of a poem needs careful preparation and is typically based on a written text. The mother may adjust her language to her child, and may be speaking *motherese*, using simplified language and repetitions such as 'who's the little baba, baba-baba?' A lecturer may be inclined to use formal language when answering student questions, yet we would probably find a few pauses, false starts and hesitations in the lecturer's language use.

In the same way, written language can take many different forms: the language in our written poem will differ from emails, textbooks and instruction manuals. Some people consider the most worthy language to be the written form. Their argument would be that in this form the correct grammar tends to be used and thoughts are presented coherently and clearly. It is the language of literature and science. Spoken language, on the other hand, is sometimes considered less important. Imagine someone speaking without having prepared what to say. Their language will probably contain *fillers* (such as *uhm*), false beginnings (such as *he was like – I mean, he is …*) and sometimes even 'mistakes' of the type that we would not expect to find in 'proper' written language (such as *he ain't done nothing*). Let us begin with an exercise to find out more:

Exercise 2.1

First, write a few lines about what you are planning to eat for dinner at the weekend. A few lines should suffice, even if all you say is that you have not made any plans yet. Next, use your mobile or other recording device to record yourself speaking for about a minute by talking about what you had for breakfast. Then replay what you recorded and write it down word by word, exactly the way it was said. Whenever there are hesitations or when you begin a sentence, change your mind and use other words, write all that down. You may be creative in your notation.

Finally, compare the written and the spoken text. In which ways does your spoken text differ from the written statement? Would you ever write a text the way you spoke? Alternatively, do you think you would ever speak a text in exactly the same way it was written?

I did the same exercise, and here are my two texts:

1 What I am planning to eat for dinner at the weekend (written text)
   Since we will have visitors this weekend, we will probably eat something nice like chicken in a creamy white wine sauce with rice and garden vegetables, most likely a mixture of spinach, swiss chard and cavalo nero from our garden, all of which are ready to harvest at the moment.

2 What I had for breakfast (spoken text)[1]
   Uh for my breakfast this morning I had uhm muesli and uhm some Weetabix as well and uh I usually eat uh my muesli with uh soy milk, so I had soy milk [falling intonation] uhm with it. And then to drink I had a cup of tea with uh milk, which is uh what I like in the morning and uhm right after that I had a cup of coffee eh black coffee, which is how I like to drink my coffee, and that's it.

My two texts differ quite a lot, in that the written text is more eloquent, flows well and is thought through. The spoken text contains quite a few hesitations (*uh* and *uhm*). There do not seem to be many 'full stops'. Rather, the speech is interspersed with discourse markers. This is not particularly eloquent, you may argue, and definitely not how someone would write, yet it is typical of spoken language. If we become very good at the art of speaking, *rhetoric*, we may be able to speak a text similar to how it would be written. This can be quite difficult. For example, in the exercise above, I thought about what I wanted to say prior to recording the spoken text. Nonetheless, my text was full of hesitations and false starts. You may have experienced something similar in your spoken text.

We can say that the written language is much 'neater' than the spoken language, mainly because we have more time to process what we are saying. Any short hesitations that are typical of spoken language (*uh*) would not normally be written down. Also, we can continuously edit our writing to make the text flow better. This is not possible in real-time spoken language.

Does this mean that written language is the 'true' language and spoken language is merely a bad representation of this underlying form? Looking at how language developed, the underlying, most basic, form of language is the spoken form. There is one reason for this: it was there first. In many ways, writing is merely a reflection of the spoken language, and by no means perfect. It may be less messy than spoken language in that false starts are eradicated and fillers are generally not written down. Yet, this is merely because the person writing the text will probably have had more time to think about what they were writing and how to communicate most efficiently.

There are also some *informal* forms of written communication that come much closer to the spoken language from the exercise above, for example the language of online chat forums. In these cases, less attention may be paid to correct wording and spelling. Still, some features typical of spoken language do not appear. Thus, a filler like *uhm* is usually not written, at least not with the same frequency with which it appears in the spoken language. Meaningful pauses may be flagged up in other ways, by punctuation, emoticons or the like. Another informal type of written communication is *textspeak*, which disregards orthographical norms to make messages more efficient, easier to type or altogether shorter, for example *how r u* and *c u l8r* instead of 'How are you?' and 'See you later'.

These types of informal written communication may have one or more of the following characteristics:

- free or innovative orthography (spelling)

- informal grammar

- less complex grammar

- use of typography (the way in which things are written down, for example bold print) to express emotions or highlights.

Exercise 2.2

Look at the following – only subtly different – types of written language from the Internet. Both are from an online forum on Scuba diving, discussing a piece of equipment called a *yellow DSMB*. Text A is an introduction to this type of equipment (cited from an official source by one of the forum users), while B is part of a comment from another forum user. Compare these two texts in their scope and formality: which one is more formal than the other? In which ways do the two excerpts differ?[2]

A An official description of the piece of equipment cited by one of the contributors:
   Yellow SMB What does it mean?

> *To some a Yellow DSMB is used exactly as an Orange one, i.e. it is used to indicate the position and presence of divers. However in growing diving circles, particularly technical diving, it has become established as an emergency signal, to communicate to the surface that the diver below has a problem of some description.*
>
> *This could mean for example that he has simply lost his Orange DSMB or perhaps more importantly that he has insufficient gas to complete the planned dive without risking an early ascent to the surface and needs help.*

B   FORUM text (on the same subject)

> *Good call, this is too important a topic to get 'lost' in another thread.*
>
> *BK I am not going to disagree with you on this one but lets remember that may shops do not differentiate between colours when selling them. Infact reputable British Manufacturers like AP Valves manufacture and sell the bicolured ones to the UK market.*
>
> *On shallow dives I have never seen yellow being a problem but somewhere like Scapa where you have a large number of technical divers (many of who will have a prepared drop tank on the boat) it certainly is causing unnecessary confusion. Infact last time we were there a techie instructor/student nearly got a tank dropped to them by us when 'practicing' yellow deployment on a 45m wreck that we had divers on.*

You may have found that text A is a more formal type of written language, using formal words like *indicate* and *presence*, quite long sentences, correct spelling and standard grammar. The forum text, on the other hand, shows a less standardized orthography, such as *infact*, grammar such as *who* instead of *whom*, some typos e.g. *may* instead of *many* and shorter sentences. The text uses typical spoken language elements like *good call* and typographic signs to highlight elements, e.g. 'lost', as well as use of words like *techie instructor*.

2.3 SIGN LANGUAGES

So far, we have considered two channels of language use: written and spoken language. Another way in which language can be transmitted is through signs. In this way, deaf communities use sign languages. Similar to spoken languages, there are many different sign languages in the world, some of which are related.

Again, like spoken languages, sign languages have grammatical structures and words. Yet, the way sign language grammar is organized is somewhat different from spoken language, in part because of the way sign language is expressed. For example, a person signing can make use of the space around them to express elements in the context. Thus, some concepts like keeping track of various characters in a story can be arranged by the signer in the physical space around them.

Sign languages are full-fledged languages and are used to communicate just like other language. Yet, there are also other ways in which signs can be used to accompany speech, such as through gestures. You probably know people who use extensive gestures when they speak. Gestures can underline and highlight certain aspects of the communication, and add additional expression to what is said. Signs can also facilitate communication where the spoken language is restricted, such as in noisy situations or across distances. Sometimes, people with limited speaking abilities can make use of signs, such as very young or disabled speakers. In these cases, signs can be taught to facilitate communication.

It has become popular among parents to join so-called baby-signing classes where babies from approximately six months old start to learn using signs in order to express their needs. Studies of deaf children learning sign language have shown that these children start to use signs at a much earlier stage than children learning to speak start to vocalize their first words. The reason for this is that motor skills needed for signing develop earlier than vocal skills. Having the capacity to express their needs through signs, babies can be less prone to experiencing frustrations than those not learning to use sign language.

The following data come from a mother using a simplified version of sign language with her baby daughter, alongside regular spoken language. The signs were used for particular requests or concepts relevant to the baby. For example, the mother started using the sign for 'milk' (opening and closing a fist, as if milking a cow) from when the baby was very young, hoping her daughter would be able to ask for milk at nursery. And true enough, the child started to use this sign when she was seven months old. At nine months, the baby picked up her next sign 'friends' (shaking hands in front of the body) from an older baby. From then on the mother attempted to use signs consistently alongside spoken language in her everyday life and the baby soon picked up signs for *cat, dog, horse, cow* and so on. At 13 months she had a developmental leap, learning new signs every day. At the same time she was vocalizing her first pre-words (such as *be* for 'bird'). By 15 months she was actively using more than 100 signs. Over the following months, as her speaking improved, she gradually stopped signing. Only sometimes, when trying to make herself understood, did she resort to signs to emphasize what she wanted to say.

Exercise 2.3

These are the signs the baby actively used at 15 months old. What do these signs have in common? Why do you think these signs were learnt rather than other possible words? A slash / indicates that the sign is used for more than one meaning.

All gone, apple, baby, ball, balloon, bath, bed, bee, beetle, bicycle, bird, biscuit, blue (not always used appropriately), *boat, book, brush teeth, bus, butterfly, cake, car, cat, change nappy, chicken, clock, close, cow, crocodile, cuddle, deer/reindeer, dinosaur, dog, doll, donkey, down, downstairs, drink, duck, eat, elephant, fish, flower, friend, frog, garden/playground, giraffe, good, goodbye, hat, helicopter/ dragonfly, hello, hippo, home, horse, hot, hurt/pain, kiss, light, lion/tiger, listen, milk, monkey, more, motorbike, mouse, no, open, out/outside, parrot, pig, plane, play, please, put on shoes, rabbit, rain, red* (not always used appropriately), *sheep, shoes, sign, sing, sit, slide, snake, star, swings, teddy, thank you, tired, to fly, toys/ play, tractor, tree, up, upstairs, what, where, who.*

The baby also used signs for the following people and characters: *Mummy, Daddy,* a number of other signs for specific friends and family, *Iggle Piggle* (signing the letter i; this is a character from a television series), *Makka Pakka* (clapping hands; this is a character from a television series who claps hands), *Upsy Daisy* (flower sign; this is a character from a television series who looks like a flower).

In the above exercise, the signs the baby knew at 15 months were probably in the input, which means that most of these signs must have been used by the parents to refer to everyday items in the baby's surroundings. Some signs point to special interests, for example there are many signs for animals. Most signs refer to everyday actions (change nappy, go upstairs, etc.) or refer to items in the world (nouns, see chapter 4). Interestingly, things (nouns) and actions (verbs) are not always distinguished. Thus, the sign for *pain* is the same as the sign for *to hurt*. In the same way, *toys* and *play* are expressed in the same way.

2.4 OTHER WAYS OF EXPRESSING LANGUAGE

Language is not just spoken, written and signed. There are other ways in which we can express ourselves. Think about the sound *tut* (or *tsk*), which is common in many cultures. Its overall meaning differs from place to place. In some areas of the world, it means 'approval'. In British culture, it is used to express dissatisfaction with a situation. For example, a person jumping a queue would generally be 'tutted' at in a British context. Like other features of language, such sounds, as well as gestures, are culturally determined. In some cultures, shaking the head means 'no', while in others it means 'yes'. Just as with the words of a language, we have to understand the context in which specific sounds and gestures are used in order to understand their meaning.

Whistling can also express linguistic signs, such as getting someone's attention. Yet, some languages make use of whistling to communicate in similar ways to spoken language. The Pirahã of the Amazon in Brazil are a small indigenous group of approximately 500 people. They have various channels for using their language, which can be spoken, shouted, hummed or whistled to convey different meanings. Whistling, for example, is used in the context of hunting, where the whistling sound can be used to coordinate efforts among the group without having to speak, and thereby sounding like birds, not warning the animals of their presence. It is possible to whistle Pirahã, because this language has both long and short <u>vowels</u> (discussed in chapter 3).

Furthermore, it is a so-called tonal language. Other tonal languages include many East Asian languages, such as Thai. A way to describe what happens in these languages is that they make use of pitch to distinguish words. Thus, in Thai, the word *mai* means 'mile' when pronounced neutrally. With a low tone (i.e. a lower pitch) *mài* the meaning is 'new', with a high tone *mái* it becomes a *question* marker at the end of a clause, such as 'right?' in English. There are also tones that are like little melodies in either rising or falling as a sound is uttered. A falling tone in Thai (like a glide from high to low) turns *mâi* into the *negation* marker 'no', and with a rising tone *mǎi* it means 'silk'. Thus, what looks like one word in English has five totally unrelated meanings in Thai, simply by the 'tones' with which it is pronounced.

2.5 SPOKEN AND ENDANGERED LANGUAGES

As we established above, the spoken and signed forms of languages are the underlying forms of language, while the written form is a secondary development. We get further evidence for the primacy of the spoken language by looking at the languages spoken in the world today. We can estimate that there are between 6,000 and 7,000 languages, but not even half of these are regularly used in their written form. Indeed, many languages do not even have writing systems or if they do, only select people have access to writing the languages. Often such languages are used among indigenous groups and small communities. In many cases the speakers know other languages as well and they may use those other languages for writing and in other formal environments. The indigenous, spoken, languages on the other hand are mostly used in informal situations, in the home, with family and among friends. Many of these languages are highly endangered, which means that they are in danger of disappearing.

Languages can become endangered and 'die' by the last speakers dying without passing on their language. The other members of the indigenous group may start to use another, bigger language associated with power and success to communicate and the indigenous language will, eventually, cease to be used.

2.6 THE NUMBER OF LANGUAGES IN THE WORLD

Exercise 2.4

Above I mentioned that there are between 6,000 and 7,000 languages spoken in the world today. Why, do you think, is it not possible to be more specific (e.g. saying that there are exactly 6,453 languages)?

So, how many languages are there in the world? There are a number of answers to this question, for the following reasons. First, it can be difficult to establish what a language is. For example, should we count British and American English as two different languages, or as different varieties of the same language? They are, after all, mostly mutually intelligible, which means that speakers of either variety understand the other. However, there are some lexical and even grammatical differences between the two. For example, not all speakers of British English would understand the American term *capsicum* for a vegetable, using *pepper* instead.

Whichever way we decide to treat British and American English, it gets even more complicated when looking at other languages. For example, many Scandinavian languages (in particular Swedish, Norwegian and Danish) are mutually intelligible in their written form, while when spoken, people less familiar with the other varieties may struggle to understand what is said. Should we, then, treat these as separate languages, or as dialects of the same language? They are spoken in separate countries, so we may decide that it is best to treat these as three separate languages.

What about languages spoken within the same country, showing a similar level of variation as the Scandinavian languages? The indigenous Sami languages spoken within Sweden (and some neighbouring countries), for example, vary to such an extent that speakers of varieties that are not geographically close can find it difficult to communicate with each other in their languages. Should these varieties be treated as separate languages, although they are not the main languages of nation states? Furthermore, let us look at the example of Bolivia. The official language is Spanish, spoken by almost all people in the country. Two indigenous languages, Aymara and Quechua, are spoken by very large numbers of speakers and are also used in writing by members of the community. There are another 30 or so indigenous languages in Bolivia, most of which are purely spoken, or only written by few members of their communities. Some of these languages are related and mutually intelligible. Others, such as Canichana, Chiquitano, Itonama and Movima are not related to any other languages, as far as we know. The fact that they are unrelated to any other languages ought to be a good reason to treat them as separate languages, despite their very small numbers of speakers and their status as purely spoken varieties. When we look in some more detail at Canichana, we find that it is actually not really spoken any more, but has largely been given up in favour of Spanish. Some people in the Canichana community still remember specific words of the language. Yet, the language has more or less disappeared, and could, in reality, be described as a 'dead' language. Should it still be counted as a language in our overall count, because some speakers still remember individual words in the language?

There are no definite answers to these questions, and for that reason it is very difficult to establish how many languages there really are in the world.

2.7 WRITING DOWN SPOKEN LANGUAGES

Like some of the indigenous languages discussed above, English was also once a purely spoken language, which was then written down by a few, select people.

When spoken languages are first written down, the orthography tends not to be standardized and there can be quite a lot of flexibility in the spelling. Standardized writing can make it easier for speakers to access texts, and thus once a language starts to be used in print media, the spelling usually becomes established and standardized. Once such conventions arise, it can be very difficult to change them, even if the spoken language has changed considerably. Language users tend to be conservative in their writing, while less restricted in speaking. For this reason, writing systems can reflect a previous state of affairs in a language. This is the case in English. For example, *knight* is no longer pronounced with a /k/ at the beginning, even though it used to be in the past (hence the spelling). All languages, even big and highly standardized languages like English, undergo change. Languages are dynamic beasts, and within a few thousand, sometimes a few hundred, years, languages can change so much that older stages of the same language become unintelligible.

Exercise 2.5

The following texts show the Lord's Prayer, a part of the Bible, translated into *Old English*, *Middle English*, Early Modern English and *Modern English*.[3] Compare the different forms of the language. Would you have been able to understand the Old English version of the text without the help of the later translations?

(Old English, around the year 1000)

Fæder ure þu þe eart on heofonum; si þin nama gehalgod; tobecume þin rice gewurþe þin willa; on eorðan swa swa on heofonum; urne gedæghwamlican hlaf syle us to dæg; and forgyf us ure gyltas; swa swa we forgyfað urum gyltendum; and ne gelæd þu us on costnunge; ac alys us of yfele soþlice.

(Middle English, around the year 1380)

Oure fadir þat art in heuenes halwid be þi name; þi reume or kyngdom come to be. Be þi wille don in herþe as it is doun in heuene. yeue to us today oure eche dayes bred. And foryeue to us oure dettis þat is oure synnys as we foryeuen to oure dettouris þat is to men þat han synned in us. And lede us not into temptacion but delyuere us from euyl.

(Early Modern English, around the year 1560)

Our father which art in heauen, hallowed be thy name. Thy kingdom come. Thy will be done in earth as it is in heauen. Giue us this day our daily bread. And forgiue us our debts as we forgiue our debters. And lead us not into temptation, but deliuer us from euill. Amen.

(Modern English, present day)

Our Father in Heaven, let your holy name be known, let your kingdom come, and your will be done, on earth as in heaven. Give us today the bread that we need, and forgive us our wrongs, as we forgive those who have done wrong to us. Do not lead us into trial, but save us from evil.

You will probably have noticed that the earlier stages of this prayer can be quite difficult to understand without knowing the context of the words and constructions used. You may also notice the development of a standard in writing, which is not fully developed in the earlier translations.

Language change tends to happen in the less standardized, informal varieties of language. Informal styles such as slang can become commonplace over time, while other elements may disappear from the language because they cease to be used. With the history of English in mind, this type of change is difficult to avoid. Rather than dismissing such changes as negative developments, we should perhaps embrace them, or at least treat them as inherent features of language. This is what most linguists do, in taking a *descriptive (grammar)* perspective to language.

2.8 PRESCRIPTIVE VERSUS DESCRIPTIVE APPROACHES TO LANGUAGE

Linguists are generally interested in the way speakers use their language, or even the way speakers judge what they can or cannot say in a language. This is called the descriptive approach to language, describing the phenomenon rather than telling speakers how to act. Most linguists do not care much about whether or not a construction or word exists in a dictionary. Rather, they are interested in the ways in which speakers use their language.

The other approach, with which most people seem much more familiar, is the *prescriptive (grammar)* approach to language. This approach prescribes to speakers a certain way of acting, following the standardizations or conventions of language. The prescriptive approach can be useful when learning a second language. In order to learn a language, you need to access the 'rules' of that language. Sometimes friends or colleagues from different fields apologize to me for their poor language use, saying that as a linguist I ought to be shocked at their way of speaking or writing. However, it is rather the other way around. Linguists rarely take a prescriptive view of language, as to 'how it ought to be according to the rules'. Rather, we look at language descriptively as to 'what speakers of the languages actually do'.

Approaches to language are very different, depending on whether they are predominantly prescriptive or descriptive. For example, most books in linguistics will describe what speakers do, taking a descriptive approach, while many books aimed at improving learners' proficiency in a language or teaching them to 'speak correctly' will be predominantly prescriptive in nature.

2.9 SUMMARY: HOW TO DEFINE *LANGUAGE*?

We have now arrived at a stage where we can try to summarize what language is: we saw above that it can be expressed through various channels, spoken, written and signed, or even hummed and whistled or thought. Primarily, language is based on the spoken (or signed) word, while writing is a newer invention. Written language is often standardized in highly formal environments, yet it can show traits of the spoken language in less formal writing styles. It is not always easy to establish how many languages there are in the world, as some languages are closely related, and even mutually intelligible. Other languages become endangered and are given up in favour of others.

In the following chapters, I will shed light on a number of features of language, for example the way in which languages are organized in terms of their sounds, grammar and meaning.

FURTHER READING

For a long time, linguists have come up with definitions of language, sometimes in the form of books aptly entitled 'Language'. These often focus on specific aspects of language from the perspective of each author, and give very different definitions of what language is. Once you have an understanding of the basics of linguistics, you may find it interesting to compare different approaches to language and to read more about the history of the field. You may want to look at books about the history of the field, such as Allan (2010) *The western classical tradition in linguistics*, which not only sheds light on the history of linguistics, but also shows links between the different approaches to language from Ancient Greece to modern theories of linguistics.

For a general introduction to language, the differences between human language and other forms of communication, see Yule (2014) *The study of language*. This book is a general introduction to linguistics and language and provides a good and accessible overview to a wide range of areas within the field.

If you want to go into some more detail with how language evolved, you will find a wide range of books dealing with these issues. A good overview is Hurford (2014) *Language origins*. As with definitions of language above, there are many different perspectives. Especially since the evolution of language is one of the things we cannot easily test, there is room for some speculation. A number of authors look at animal communication to understand how language has developed, for example Fitch (2010) *The evolution of language*. Others draw on a wide range of sources, including the way children acquire language, such as Tomasello (2010) *Origins of human communication*. The evolution of language in relation to use of gestures is treated by McNeill (2012) *How language began: gesture and speech in human evolution*. An overview of different approaches to the evolution of language is Tallerman (2005, ed.) *The origins of language*, which includes chapters written by scholars with different perspectives on how language developed, giving a broad overview of the field.

The differences between spoken and written language are commonly dealt with in the study of discourse analysis, which I will look at in chapter 7. The background of how spoken English was first written down is treated in a number of books on the history of the language, such as Baugh & Cable (2012) *A history of the English language*.

There is a lot of literature about gestures and sign language, including Kendon (2004) *Gesture* and Sutton-Spence & Woll (1999) *The linguistics of British sign language*. *Baby signing*, however, has only recently attracted academic interest, alongside its rise in popularity among parents. There are a number of articles about the topic, such as Doherty-Sneddon (2008) *The great baby signing debate: academia meets public interest.*

To read more about the languages of the world, you can have a look at the Ethnologue (http://www.ethnologue.com = Lewis *et al.* 2014). This is a website put together by the missionary organization *SIL*. Originally this list was intended to give an overview of which languages still 'needed' Bible translations, with the aim to translate the Bible into as many languages as possible. However, it is also a helpful resource to gain an overview of different languages and language families. Another online resource is Glottolog (http://www.glottolog.org). A treatment of different language families can also be found in Pereltsvaig (2012) *The languages of the world: an introduction.*

For similarities and differences between the structures of the languages of the world, Dryer & Haspelmath (2013) *The world atlas of language structures online* provides an overview of a wide range of linguistic structures (including sounds, grammar and other features) across a sample of languages of the world. The information can be accessed through wals.info.

For endangered languages have a look at Evans (2010) *Dying words: endangered languages and what they have to tell us* and Austin & Sallabank (2011, eds.) *The Cambridge handbook of endangered languages.* For saving endangered languages and linguistic fieldwork, Sakel & Everett (2012) *Linguistic fieldwork* gives an account of how languages can be described and analysed. Everett's (2009) *Don't sleep, there are snakes* is a personal account of working on the indigenous language Pirahã in the Brazilian Amazon, first as a missionary, and later as a linguist. Another personal account is Harrison's (2010) *The last speakers: the quest to save the world's most endangered languages.*

NOTES

1   The sound file of the spoken text can be accessed through the companion website at LINK.
2   Both texts are taken from the following forum: http://www.ukdivers.com/community/threads/the-yellow-dsmb-and-its-use.780/ [accessed 13.6.2012].
3   These translations are taken from the website http://www.prayer.su, which features many other translations of the same text [accessed 27.8.2014].

3

Sounds

IN THIS CHAPTER

This chapter deals with the sounds of languages, a topic usually referred to as phonetics. The study of phonetics is about sounds and their features, as well as the representation of sounds in the International Phonetics Alphabet (_IPA_). In this chapter I will also look at features that go beyond individual sounds, such as intonation, and briefly introduce the study of phonology. In particular, this chapter encompasses:

- Spoken language

- Differences between sounds

- IPA (International Phonetics Alphabet)

- Vowels

- Consonants

- Phonemes and the study of phonology.

3.1 SPOKEN LANGUAGE

In the previous chapter, we saw that the written and the spoken language can be quite different. While the written language is, in principle, a representation of the spoken language, the way words are pronounced does not always correspond to the way they are written. When we look at the written language, we can be led to believe that the spoken language also consists of separate words, chunks of 'noise' broken up at the word boundaries. And in very carefully pronounced language that is sometimes the case. But what happens in 'normal' spoken language?

Exercise 3.1

Listen again to the recording you made in chapter 2: is there a break at the beginning and end of each word, or do you find larger chunks of words pronounced together?

You may have used quite careful and slow speech in your recording, because you were aware of being recorded at the time and subconsciously made an effort in the way you were speaking. Yet, even in this case, there are probably a number of words in your recording that are pronounced together as chunks. In my recording[1] *my breakfast this morning uhm* appears to be pronounced as one long chunk of speech, rather than each word pronounced on its own. Some elements that are regularly contracted in the spoken language, such as *it's* and *don't*, have even made it into the written form.

In this chapter, we are going to explore the sounds that make up words and longer chunks of spoken language. The written form of English is not merely a past representation of the language, but also an approximation covering for a range of different dialects and pronunciations.

Exercise 3.2

Try to describe, as clearly as you can, how the following words are pronounced, in particular the letter /a/ that appears in each case.

a   bad

b   late

c   hard

d   Manchester

You can record yourself or a native speaker of English pronouncing these words. You can also use the 'forvo' website, which is a collection of pronunciations submitted by speakers of different languages, where you will be able to find variations in the pronunciation as well.

When you listen to *bad*, *late* and *hard* pronounced by speakers of British English, you will realize that the sounds represented by /a/ in writing can actually be very different sounds. While native speakers may not be aware of this, learners of English often struggle with such differences in pronunciation. When we look at how people from different dialectal backgrounds pronounce some of these words, we can see even greater variation, for example the /a/ in *Manchester* pronounced by a speaker from southern England may sound very different from that of a speaker from Manchester.

Spelling does not necessarily help much in this case, so we have to find other ways to describe the differences between these sounds, for example when teaching English pronunciation to speakers of other languages or when we want to describe the features of certain dialects. For this, we need the IPA, which stands for International Phonetics Alphabet. In this alphabet (as opposed to English spelling), each letter represents a unique sound. So when we write something down in IPA, it means others will be able to replicate exactly how what we wrote down was pronounced.

In the IPA, our /a/ sounds from above would be written as follows:

bad [bæd]
late [leɪt]
hard [hɑːd]

I presented the IPA symbols in square brackets []. This is the typical notation for the IPA, a convention among linguists. To simplify it, we could say that the letters that appear between these slashes // are pretty much the same as would appear in writing.[2]

In the example, the first vowel in *Manchester* would be written [æ] when pronounced by someone from the South and [a] when pronounced by a speaker from the North of the UK. A simple written /a/ can be pronounced in many different ways. Crucially, such differences in pronunciation do not contrast in meaning, but only tell us something about the background of the speaker. In other cases there are differences in pronunciation that lead to changes in meaning. For example *mat* [mæt] (pronounced [mat] by a speaker from the North) and *mate* [meɪt]. In this case, what looks like the same vowel in spelling /a/ leads to differences in meaning. I will return to such contrasts below.

For now, let us consider why the IPA is useful. In the examples so far it helped us to differentiate between different pronunciations, which were not always apparent in the spelling. Indeed, anybody trained in the IPA would know the pronunciation of [meɪt], while this would not be the case if they were not speakers of English and were presented with the spelling *mate*. Knowing the IPA is useful when learning other languages, especially those with opaque orthographies like English.

We find similar variation to /a/ above in other letters of the English alphabet. If we consider all languages of the world there are many more sounds and variations to take into account. We could imagine that it would be quite complex to map all of the sounds in the world's languages using the IPA. Yet, while there certainly are special, rare sounds in some languages, most sounds across languages are rather straightforward and are easily mapped using the IPA. Rather than having to learn many different symbols, there is a subset of around a hundred or so symbols that make up the most common sounds across the globe.

You may have to learn a subset of IPA symbols as part of your degree. Not all linguists regularly use even these symbols, let alone the entire IPA. For many linguists it is sufficient to be able to recognize the IPA when they encounter it and to know where to look for further information on the pronunciation. Let us now look at some of the common sounds in the IPA. I will consider vowels and consonants one after the other.

3.2 VOWELS

The following vowel chart, sometimes also called *vowel triangle* or probably more appropriately 'vowel quadrilateral' shows different possible vowel sounds:

Figure 3.1
IPA, vowels

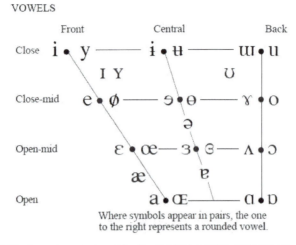

Source: IPA Chart, http://www.langsci.ucl.ac.uk/ipa/ipachart.html, available under a Creative Commons Attribution-Sharealike 3.0 Unported License. Copyright © 2005 International Phonetic Association.

To understand how this triangle works, let us start to look at the way in which the sounds are organized within it.

Imagine you are tasked with brushing a child's teeth. You ask her to make a sound, which maximally opens her mouth. Which vowel would be most appropriate to use: [a], [e], [i], [u] or [o]?

Now, your answer was probably [a]. This sound is a typical 'open' vowel, and is furthermore pronounced at the front of the mouth. The mouth has to be open; to see what I mean, try to pronounce with your mouth firmly closed. If we pronounce [a] and slowly close the mouth further towards a smile, we move through a range of vowels towards [e] and ultimately [i], which is sometimes written /ee/ in English. In this case the teeth are relatively close together. Indeed, in our tooth-brushing exercise we could ask the child to say [i] in order to brush the fronts of the teeth more easily. In short, the vowels at the top of the triangle are closed; the vowels at the bottom are open.

The other scale within the vowel triangle is from left to right, ranging from front to back vowels. Some vowels are pronounced at the front of the tongue, while others appear further back. Try to say [i] and [u] or [e] and [o]. Where is each of these vowels pronounced?

Finally, for the sake of completeness, we can look at the way the IPA for vowels represents the roundedness of the lips. In the IPA rounded vowels are given to the right in the lines in the triangle; unrounded vowels are given to the left of these lines. That means [a] is unrounded, [ɶ] is pronounced in exactly the same place, just with the lips rounded. In English, some vowels are pronounced with rounded lips, while others are unrounded, yet there is no contrast in meaning between the two types. French and German, on the other hand, have a contrast between rounded and unrounded vowels.

For example the unrounded front vowel [i] and the rounded front vowel [y] contrast different meanings in German words such as *für* 'for' [fy:ɐ̯] and *vier* 'four' [fiːɐ̯], where [y] is a rounded vowel and [i] is pronounced in the same place but is unrounded.

At the very centre of the triangle is a vowel that exists in many languages, but which is not always written as such. This is the 'lazy' vowel *Schwa* [ə]. It appears in English when a syllable is not stressed, such as the /a/ in *about* or the /e/ in *given*. Try to pronounce these words and notice how de-focused the /a/ and /e/ are in these cases. There is no need to produce the full vowel qualities, and a 'lazy', centralized pronunciation of the 'vowel elements' is sufficient.

Finally, there are combinations of vowels, such as the other vowels in *about* [ə'baʊt] and the pronunciation of *late* [leɪt] discussed above. These are called *diphthongs*, and they combine two qualities of vowels. The /aʊ/ in about, for example starts in and moves gradually into [ʊ]. That is, if you consult the vowel triangle above, it starts as a front open vowel and moves further back in the direction of closed back vowels. Note also the lip rounding change in /aʊ/. As before, try to pronounce it yourself to understand how this 'movement' happens.

3.3 CONSONANTS

With a little practice, it becomes easy to pronounce different types of vowels; at least, that is, easier than pronouncing consonants. That is primarily so because vowels can appear on their own, without the need of other elements being present. Consonants, on the other hand, generally need to appear together with vowels to be heard. Furthermore, when analysing consonants it is not enough merely to look at the position of the tongue. We will also have to look at the type of airflow from the lungs.

As we speak, the first thing that happens is that air travels out of our lungs to the *larynx* (see figure 3.2). This is the home of the *vocal cords*. They will become important in a short while, but for now let us move further up the throat. When the air has passed the vocal cords, it moves towards the *uvula*, that little protrusion between your tonsils you can see when opening your mouth wide. Then, the air reaches the *velum*, which is also called the soft palate at the back of your mouth. You can feel the velum with the tip of your tongue if you move your tongue back along your palate.

The back of the velum is a place of choice for the airflow: air can either move largely through the nasal cavity (i.e. the nose), in which case we get *nasal consonants* like [n] or [m], or the air can move through the oral cavity towards the mouth, producing *oral consonants*. To understand how this happens, try to pronounce [f] and [m]. You will find that you can close your lips while pronouncing [m], while this is not possible with [f], where air has to travel through the lips.

The next step on our journey is the *hard palate*, i.e. the bony area at the top of your mouth. Then comes the *alveolar ridge*, the bony ridge right behind the teeth. Finally, there are the teeth (producing *dental* sounds) and the lips (producing *labial* sounds). These are referred to as the places of articulation, shown in figure 3.2.

Not just the place of articulation defines a consonant, but also the manner in which the air travels makes a difference to the resulting sound. For example, there are sounds

Figure 3.2
Places of articulation

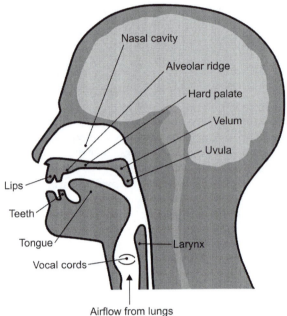

Source: Illustration by Patrick Thornhill, used with permission.

that require a short 'explosion', such as [p] and [t]. These sounds are momentary; they cannot be sustained over a long period of time. Try to hold a [t] for five seconds. Now try to hold a [s] for five seconds. The latter is possible, as this is a different type of sound making use of friction. When pronouncing [s], the tongue is restricting the airflow, making the airflow pass a 'barrier'. As long as there is enough air coming from the lungs, the consonant can be sustained. The two types discussed so far are the main types of 'manner of articulation'. [t] and [p], i.e. those with the minor 'explosion', are aptly called _plosives_. Consonants such as [s] and others in which friction plays a role are called _fricatives_. There are further manners of articulation. These include _nasals_, where the main airflow is through the nasal cavity, _trills_, in which tongue or lips are 'rolled', and _laterals_ in which the airflow is restricted to the sides of the tongue.

The IPA for consonants[3] takes into account both the place of articulation (along the top of the table from left to right), as well as the manner of articulation (arranged in the left-hand column of the table). It is shown in figure 3.3 below.

There is one additional distinction captured in the consonantal IPA chart by presenting two consonants within the same cell in the table: the left consonant is _voiceless_ and the right consonant _voiced_. This distinction is produced at the vocal cords. The vocal cords can be open or partially shut; the latter means that air is forced through, making the vocal cords vibrate. When that happens, the sound produced is

Figure 3.3
IPA, consonants

THE INTERNATIONAL PHONETIC ALPHABET (revised to 2005)

CONSONANTS (PULMONIC)   © 2005 IPA

	Bilabial	Labiodental	Dental	Alveolar	Postalveolar	Retroflex	Palatal	Velar	Uvular	Pharyngeal	Glottal
Plosive	p b			t d		ʈ ɖ	c ɟ	k ɡ	q ɢ		ʔ
Nasal	m	ɱ		n		ɳ	ɲ	ŋ	N		
Trill	B			r					R		
Tap or Flap		ѵ̆		ɾ		ɽ					
Fricative	ɸ β	f v	θ ð	s z	ʃ ʒ	ʂ ʐ	ç ʝ	x ɣ	χ ʁ	ħ ʕ	h ɦ
Lateral fricative				ɬ ɮ							
Approximant		ʋ		ɹ		ɻ	j	ɰ			
Lateral approximant				l		ɭ	ʎ	L			

Where symbols appear in pairs, the one to the right represents a voiced consonant. Shaded areas denote articulations judged impossible.

voiced. When the air flows freely through the vocal cords, the sound is *voiceless*. Try to hold your throat while pronouncing /s/ and /z/ (try to avoid pronouncing them together with any vowels, but just on their own). What can you feel in each case? In which case do the vocal cords vibrate, i.e. which of the two is voiced and which one is voiceless? The reason to avoid vowels is that they are generally all voiced, while consonants can be voiced or voiceless.

You can read the IPA consonant chart in the following way. If you are interested in consonants produced near the alveolar ridge behind the teeth, you can go to the (dental) alveolar (postalveolar) column in the table and look for different manners of articulation in the rows below, such as:

- a plosive (the tongue is on the alveolar ridge, fully closing the oral tract. Pressure builds up behind it as the air comes through the lungs, and is suddenly released. The resulting sound is a [t] or a [d] if the vocal cords vibrated, i.e. if it is voiced).

- a nasal (the tongue rests on the alveolar ridge, and the air is passed through the nasal cavity. The resulting sound is a [n]).

- a fricative (the tongue is placed on the alveolar ridge, but there is a little space in the middle through which the air (from the lungs) can be pressed. The resulting sound is a [s] or if voiced a [z]).

Exercise 3.3

We can now try to find stops, nasals and fricatives produced in other places.

Try to produce the following:

a   a stop at the level of the soft palate at the far back of your mouth (a velar) – this should come out as /k/ or /g/

b   a nasal at the level of the lips (a bilabial) – this should sound like /m/

c   a fricative pronounced between your teeth and lips, such as when resting your front teeth on your lower lip (a labiodental) – this should sound like /f/ or /v/

Exercise 3.4

Try to decipher the following common English words by using the IPA tables above. You will also need to know that [ː] marks a long vowel and ['] marks the following syllable as stressed:[4]

a   [pliːz]

b   ['nʌθɪŋ]

c   [huː]

d   [prənʌnsɪ'eɪʃn]

e   [tə'mɒrəʊ]

3.4 OTHER TYPES OF PRONUNCIATION

The introduction to the IPA above covered only the most common sounds. There are other tables for the IPA dealing with less common sounds or other ways of pronunciation. For example, the symbols [ː] and ['] in the exercise above mark such additional features. One other such way of pronunciation is tones, which we discussed for Thai in chapter 2. In that chapter, the different tones for the word *mai* were given by accents on the first vowel. This is a common way of presenting tones in writing. Yet again, there is also a standardized way of dealing with tones using the IPA.

3.5 THE STUDY OF SOUNDS

Studying sounds, we do not just look at individual pronunciations, but also at the way in which languages organize their sounds. For example, sounds of the IPA can be lumped together to express different meanings, such as the different pronunciations of /a/ in English discussed above. For example, while Japanese uses tones, it treats the pronunciations of [r] and [l] as the same sound in the language, just like the different pronunciations of /a/ in English above. We say that they are variations of the same *phoneme*. Using one or the other may sound like a different dialect, but the overall meaning is still understood. In English, however, these two sounds are two phonemes in that they distinguish meaning: *rice* and *lice* are two different words. [æ] and [a], on the other hand, are variations (so-called *allophones*) of the same phoneme in English. They do not distinguish meaning, and *Manchester* pronounced with one or the other will still refer to the same place. This way in which sounds, tones and other structures interact is looked at by the study of phonology.

Furthermore, linguists look at the ways in which sounds are put together to form syllables. These small units can be built up according to different rules in different languages. Thus, in English syllables can consist of a consonant (abbreviated *C*) and a vowel (*V*), i.e. CV as in *go*. Or it can just be a V as in the words *I* or *a*. Or the syllable can have a CVC structure as in *can* or *main* (in the latter case the V in the middle is a diphthong). English also allows for *consonant clusters*, which means various consonants appearing together, for example CCCVC as in *street*. Other languages are more rigid in their syllable structures, and in many languages there are also restrictions on which specific consonants can appear at the beginning or end of a syllable.

Exercise 3.5

Look at the following data from Finnish and determine from them the syllable structure of the language. Finnish pronunciation mostly corresponds to how it is written, so all consonants written in the examples are pronounced the way they appear. Syllable boundaries are given by -. In particular, take into account the two *loanwords* from Swedish, analysing how their forms were adjusted to fit with the Finnish syllable structure:

a   *koi-ra* 'dog'

b   *ta-lo* 'house'

c   *seit-se-män* 'seven'

d   *jo-kai-nen* 'every'

e   *päi-vä* 'day'

f   *ei* 'no'

g   *Hel-sin-ki* 'Helsinki'

h   *la-si* 'glass, from Swedish *glas*'

i   *kou-lu* 'school, from Swedish *skola*'

You will probably have seen that Finnish does not allow consonant clusters within a syllable. Rather, the data suggest that Finnish has a syllable structure of (C)V(C), which means that a syllable can consist of a vowel (or diphthong – a combination of vowels), while there may or may not be a consonant at the beginning and/or the end of each syllable.

FURTHER READING

There are many excellent textbooks on phonetics and phonology, as well as copious online resources. Modern textbooks include Ashby (2011) *Understanding phonetics* and Knight (2012) *Phonetics: a coursebook*. Likewise, there is a range of textbooks with a focus on phonology, such as Gussenhoven & Jacobs (2011) *Understanding phonology*, 3rd edition. If you want to kill two birds with one stone, you can also opt for a textbook combining phonetics and phonology, such as Davenport & Hannahs (2010) *Introducing phonetics and phonology*, 3rd edition.

There are also many excellent online resources to help you learn the IPA. These include materials for teachers, such as the BBC and British Council's phonemic chart, which you can find by searching for 'phonemic chart for teaching English', as well as a website originally put together by the late Peter Ladefoged, through which you can play IPA sounds at the onset or in the middle of a word, which you will find by searching for 'Ladefoged phonetics chart'.

Many dictionaries, including some online dictionaries, give transcriptions in IPA, if you are unsure about how to do this. However, beware that the IPA transcription may refer to a different pronunciation, e.g. American English.

While the IPA can help you pronounce new words, it is not always possible to find IPA transcriptions for all words. This is where Wiki-style websites are useful, such as 'forvo', where users can pronounce words in any language of the world. You can then play their pronunciation and – for the frequent ones – get ideas of different pronunciations in different parts of the world.

NOTES

1   The recording is accessible from the companion website at LINK.
2   In reality there is some more to it. The slashes are usually used for phonemes, which are abstract units of sounds in a language, discussed briefly at the end of this chapter.
3   In this case they are consonants for which the air travels from the lungs. There are others types of consonants, and you can see information about further reading at the end of the chapter.
4   The words given here are *please, nothing, who, pronunciation* and *tomorrow*.

Word classes

IN THIS CHAPTER

This chapter looks at what words are and the different classes to which words can belong. Beginning with *word classes* in English, I will move on to word classes in other languages at the end of the chapter. The focus of this chapter is on:

- Words and dictionaries

- Nouns, verbs, adjectives, adverbs, pronouns, other word classes

- Concrete and abstract nouns

- Intransitive and transitive verbs

- Word classes in other languages.

4.1 WORDS

Let us take a closer look at 'words', before we divide them up into different classes. We may say that words are clusters of letters in texts, separated from other words by spaces. That is not a bad definition to begin with, and it holds true for the written language, at least most of the time. In the spoken language, however, especially in fast speech, 'words' can blend together, as we saw in the previous chapter. Frequent contractions of words are even represented in less formal forms of the written language, such as *isn't* as opposed to *is not*. Now the question is whether *isn't* is one word or two. It is pronounced, as well as written, as one. Yet, it has two distinct meanings and two underlying forms, which can also appear on their own. For this reason, some would probably treat it as two words grammatically. Still, this is debatable and not all would agree. Furthermore, combining two underlying meanings in one word is rather common, such as *unfair*, consisting of *fair* and the negative *un-* part.

Let us consider another example: *lol*. This is an abbreviation, giving the initial three letters of the words *laugh out loud* (or, for some older speakers, *lots of love*). Again, we could treat *lol* as a single word, or analyse it as an abbreviation of three separate words. In this case, most linguists would argue that it has become a word in its own right. There are many such *acronyms*, which means words based on the first letters of their original component parts. Sometimes speakers struggle to find the original forms, or are not even *aware* that these are acronyms.

Exercise 4.1

Do you think *laser, radar* and *dvd* are acronyms? If so, what do they stand for?[1]

There are some properties that words have in common. For example, words have meanings that individual speakers of a language recognize. Sometimes these meanings are the combined meanings of two or more underlying words. For example, the word *cherrytree* is a so-called <u>*compound*</u>, which combines two such meanings: *cherry* and *tree*. In this case, the first element *cherry* tells us something more specific about the thing we are talking about, a *tree*. While I chose to write *cherrytree* as one word, there are other ways in which compounds can be presented, such as *cherry tree* or even *cherry-tree*. There are sometimes conventions as to which of these is deemed the most 'correct'. Yet, in grammatical terms, they are all compounds, which means they are all considered one word, independent on how they are spelt.

In the case of *cherrytree*, whichever way you spell it, we have the combination of two independent words: *cherry* and *tree*. They each have a meaning, and they can appear independently, on their own. Yet, there are also cases such as *unfair* where two meanings are combined in a single word, while not all parts are words that can appear on their own. We will look at such meaningful units smaller than words in chapter 5.

Defining words in terms of meaning and 'standing alone' is just a beginning. We also have to take other clues into account, for example the prosody. Word accent can mark a single word, as opposed to two separate elements. For this, compare *green house* and *greenhouse* – in the first case each part is stressed, while in the second the word accent falls on *green-* alone. This results in different meanings.

4.2 DICTIONARIES

Words are, of course, also those elements found in dictionaries. Once a word has become sufficiently established, that is, once it is used regularly by different people in a speech community, it is usually considered for inclusion in a dictionary, such as the *Oxford English Dictionary* (short *OED*). The *OED* adds new words all the time, and in 2013 these included *FOMO* (from 'fear of missing out') and *selfie*, a word that has become very commonplace in the English language, in particular since its inclusion in the *OED*.[2] Our example from above, *lol*, is also found in the *OED*.

Yet, despite its wide scope, not all words will be found in the *OED*, or in other dictionaries, for that matter. That is because new words, just like *selfie*, are made up every day. They are used long before they get recognized in the *OED*. Indeed it is their widespread use that leads to their inclusion in the *OED* in the first place. Although they do not appear in a dictionary, we still recognize such terms as words. We can also form new constructions with new words, such as *he selfied that picture*, in which case the thing *selfie* turns into an action *he selfied*. I can imagine that you still understand what I am talking about, even though this may be the first time you heard this particular word-form being used. The reason for this is that we possess a mental *lexicon*. These are all the words an individual knows, uses, or at least is able to understand. Using this underlying knowledge of the mental lexicon, creative speakers can make up their own, new terms.

Exercise 4.2

Try to find words that are not (yet) included in the *OED*. If you do not know any such words, try to look up new slang online, such as in Wiki-type dictionaries, or online wordlists. For each of the words you found, try to establish whether they are likely to ever be included in the *OED*. Note that even swearwords are generally considered in the *OED*, so that is not a reason why they would not be included.

4.3 DIVIDING WORDS INTO CLASSES

Now that we have explored what words are, it is time to look at the different classes to which words can belong. Most languages distinguish word classes such as 'nouns', 'verbs' and 'adjectives'.[3] Nouns generally refer to things (such as *house*), verbs to actions (such as *eat*), while adjectives describe qualities (such as *beautiful*). These word classes are used in different 'places' in sentences to refer to people or things, actions and events, attributes and more. Linguists sometimes refer to word classes as *parts of speech*.

Exercise 4.3

Look around you and make a list (consisting of at least ten words) of what you see.

My list includes an *office,* a messy *desk,* a *pen,* a *computer,* a *water-bottle,* a *picture,* a *window,* my fluffy *cat,* a *tree* and my *neighbour* (through the window). All of these are things, living beings and places; and all of these words have in common that they are nouns or so-called *noun phrases*, which means combinations of nouns with other elements that give further information, such as *my* and *fluffy*. It is likely that your list will contain many noun phrases as well, as nouns are usually the easiest things to spot. It is less likely that the main words of your list are verbs (actions), for example *eat* or *adjectives* (properties) such as *pretty*. And it is highly unlikely that your list contains words belonging to yet other word classes, such as the preposition *into* or the filler *uh*.

We generally distinguish between *open word classes* and *closed word classes*. Open classes are those to which we can easily add new members, such as nouns and verbs. New nouns are invented or *borrowed* from other languages every day, such as *jeggings* (a mixture of *jeans* and *leggings*) or the vegetable *bok choy*, sometimes written *pak choi,* using a Cantonese loanword, which reflects its origin. Closed word classes are those that are much more fixed and less flexible. Introducing a new preposition to function like *at* is generally much more difficult than introducing a new noun![4]

In what follows, we will start looking at the big, open word classes first and then work our way through to the smaller, closed, classes. I will mainly use English as an example in the main part of this chapter, as word classes can vary considerably across languages. At the end of the chapter, I will discuss how word classes can be arranged in other languages.

In order to define a word class, we usually have to look at the grammatical structures with which words of specific classes appear. Again, these can differ considerably from language to language. Most of the grammar associated with word classes will be discussed in chapter 5.

4.4 NOUNS

When I was a student, a housemate of mine started to learn German. He put little stickers with words for common expressions around the house, hoping that he would eventually learn the words by repeatedly encountering them in the appropriate environments. The door to the bathroom sported a sticky-note stating *Badezimmer*, the bathroom mirror *Spiegel*, as well as *Waschbecken* ('wash basin', pointing downwards), alongside *Zahnbürste* ('toothbrush'). There must have been at least 200 sticky-notes around the house.

Exercise 4.4

Think about my friend's language learning and the success of the method described here. Can you see any shortcomings?

My friend eventually did learn German, but had he exclusively used stickers, he would probably have struggled to communicate in the language. In terms of word classes, we can be pretty sure (even without looking at all of his stickers) that most of them referred to nouns, in particular to places ('bathroom') and things ('toothbrush'). He would have found it considerably more difficult to apply stickers to verbs such as *eat*, *exercise, develop* and *overtake*, let alone sentences such as *hello, how are you* or *I walked to work today.*[5]

Even within the word class of nouns, my friend faced some restrictions: he could only physically label things, places and – to a lesser degree – living beings. He actually initially tried to put stickers on his housemates! These things, places and living beings are <u>concrete nouns</u>.[6] We can define concrete nouns as words referring to entities we can perceive using our bodily senses, in particular our eyes and ears. Yet, even within the category of concrete nouns, some are difficult to label with stickers, such as *air, fire* and *water*.

There are also other types of nouns that are much more difficult to pin down. These are *abstract nouns*, such as *happiness, mathematics, linguistics, sense* and *opportunity*.

Exercise 4.5

Look back at your list above: are the elements listed all concrete nouns or *phrases* containing concrete nouns (i.e. do they refer to things, people or places), or are there also abstract nouns among those elements?

We have seen that we can distinguish different classes of nouns, depending on whether the meaning is concrete or abstract, the latter referring to abstract entities that we cannot see, hear or sense in any other way. Thus, within the word class of nouns, we can distinguish different subcategories based on the meanings of the words. Why, then, do we refer to all of these as nouns, despite their apparent differences?

You may think this is a trivial question. Some people quite intuitively feel that *gender, dog, likeness, place, man* are all nouns, without the need for further definitions. But there are a number of cases where it is not obvious whether something is a noun. Look at the words *apple* and *home*. *Apple* is easy to spot as a noun. It is a concrete noun and you could even put a sticker on it for language-learning purposes if you wanted to. *Home*, however, is a bit more difficult to classify. It can function as a noun, but it can also have other functions. Let us take a look at the way these nouns are used.

To start with *apple*, it can be preceded by a very common word – *the*. This is a *definite article* (this is different from the *indefinite article*, another very common word – *a*). The definite article means that whatever comes afterwards is well defined in the context (I discuss articles in more detail in section 4.9 below):

(1) *the apple.*

In English, most nouns – both concrete and abstract nouns – can appear with a definite article, e.g. *the opportunity* and *the sense*. But in some cases, using a definite article with a noun appears odd. How about *the mathematics* and *the happiness*? These may sound odd to some speakers just like that, but would be fine if you add something else:

(2) *the mathematics of card tricks.*
(3) *the happiness of children.*

We can thus say that nouns appear with definite articles. Looking at *home*, this is clearly the case:

(4) *the home*
     (e.g. *The home of a famous artist*).

Home can appear with a definite article and thus appears in a similar environment as other nouns. We have thereby just carried out a test of whether or not *home* would qualify as a noun, and it passed with flying colours.

However, *home* can also belong to other word classes. In (5) *home* is used as a verb:

(5) *We are looking to home five stray cats.*

In this case, *home* appears with the infinitive marker *to* (see chapter 5 for more information on the infinitive), and is used as a verb. Yet, *home* can also be a so-called <u>adverb</u> that describes a verbal action, as in (6):

(6) *I'll take you home.*

In this case *home* refers to a place and could be replaced by *back* or *there*. Note that neither in (5) nor in (6) can *home* appear with a definite article. We indicate this by an asterisk (*) in front of the unacceptable example:

(7) **We are looking to the home five stray cats.*
(8) **I'll take you the home.*

Which word class a word belongs to thus depends on the context in which that word is used. Many words can change word class without much ado, such as *home* used as a noun, a verb and an adverb. Linguists call this phenomenon <u>conversion</u>.

Summarizing, for now we have defined nouns in terms of their meaning (linguists call that their semantics), and their grammar. In English, nouns generally appear with articles. Still, defining nouns through articles (definite or indefinite) alone is not really appropriate for all languages of the world. Many languages do not use articles, or have different means of conveying information about whether a noun is known, i.e. definite, or new or less focused on, i.e. indefinite. Hence, we need to look at other grammatical structures typical for nouns. Some of these, like plural marking, will be explored in further detail in chapter 5.

4.5 VERBS

Verbs are elements that express actions or events. In the same way as we distinguished between concrete and abstract nouns, we can find different types of verbs according to their semantics. For example, the verb *eat* is an <u>action verb</u>. It usually involves someone doing some *eating*. You may argue that eating can be rather subconscious in front of the TV in the evening, but that is up for debate. There are <u>involuntary actions</u>, such as *sneeze*. Very few people can sneeze voluntarily. Rather, this is something that just happens and cannot be controlled. Finally, there are verbs that describe <u>states</u> and <u>events</u>, such as *sleep* or *fall*. These express very different meanings from actions.

There is another way in which we can distinguish different types of verbs, and that has to do with the number of nouns, or more precisely noun phrases with which a verb can appear.[7] Some verbs appear with just one noun phrase:

(9)   *The dog barked.* (noun phrase: *the dog*)
(10)   *My father slept.* (noun phrase: *my father*)
(11)   *The man sneezed.* (noun phrase: *the man*)

Some other verbs have to appear with two noun phrases:

(12)   *Teenagers like cookies.* (noun phrases: *teenagers, cookies*)[8]
(13)   *Those cars produce a lot of pollution.* (noun phrases: *those cars, a lot of pollution*)
(14)   *John saw Mary.* (noun phrases: *John, Mary*)

Some verbs even need to appear with three noun phrases to make sense:

(15)   *John gave the cookie to Mary.* (noun phrases: *John, the cookie, Mary*)

The verbs that appear with just one noun phrase (examples 9–11) are called *intransitive verbs*, those that appear with two noun phrases (examples 12–14) are *transitive verbs* and finally those that require three noun phrases to make sense (example 15) are *ditransitive verbs*.[9] The concept of verbs appearing with a certain number of noun phrases is referred to as *transitivity*.

One way to remember this could be to think of it as a transport or *transit* system. An intransitive verb does not take you anywhere (*in-* being a negative, just like *un-*), whereas a transitive verb leads to the next noun phrase. Ditransitives lead you even further, to yet another noun phrase.

Note that some verbs can both be intransitive and transitive in different environments:

Intransitive: *I eat*
Transitive: *I eat cake*

Exercise 4.6

Look at the following verbs and decide whether they are intransitive, transitive or ditransitive: *love, read, hit, sit, sleep, sing, run.*

In this list, the following verbs are intransitive: *sit* and *sleep* (examples: *I sit, I sleep*). Transitive verbs are *love* and *hit* (examples: *I love him, I hit him*). The rest of the verbs can be used intransitively and transitively: *read, sing* and *run* (examples: *I read, I read a book; I sing, I sing a song; I run, I run a marathon*). Indeed, *read* and *sing* can also be used ditransitively, in *I read her a story* and *I sang them a song*. Indeed, note that even the intransitive verbs *sit* and *sleep* can be used transitively in the following exceptional cases: *the couch sits three, this bed sleeps two.*

Apart from the intransitive, transitive and ditransitive verbs discussed so far, there are also further ways of distinguishing verbs: a separate class of verbs are *auxiliary verbs*. These appear together with other verbs in *verb phrases*.[10] Auxiliaries are usually short words, and include *should, will, be* and *have*. They can be divided up into *modal auxiliaries* expressing things like attitudes, obligations or possibilities connected to the main verb (*mood*), such as *should buy* and *temporal-aspectual auxiliaries* giving more information about the time (*tense*), the internal structure of an action or event (*aspect*). These include words like *will, have, be* as in *will go, had come, is walking*. The categories of tense, aspect and mood will be explored in more detail in chapter 5.

We saw above that the word *home* can belong to several word classes at the same time. This exercise is about words that can be both nouns and verbs. For example, we can argue that there are two different words *hit* and *hit*. Both have the same form, but they belong to different word classes, as they are used in very different environments, even though they have related meanings:

(16)   *The hit was played on the radio.*
(17)   *I hit the wall in anger.*

In (16) *hit* is a noun. We can tell this, because it appears with an article. In (17) *hit* is expressing an action, referring to me hitting the wall. In this case *hit* is a verb, even though it has exactly the same form as the noun.[11]

Exercise 4.7

Take a look at the list of words given below and consider which of them behave like *hit* in being both nouns and verbs. Try to identify nouns as elements that can appear with an article (*the* or *a*), and verbs as elements that denote actions or events:

a   walk

b   eat

c   go

d   like

e   room

f   generate

g   employ

h   do

i   overdo

There are a number of words in the list above that can be both nouns and verbs. You may have a slightly different analysis from mine below, as some of these expressions depend on your individual dialects. *Walk* (a) is a verb in the example *I walk*, as it describes the action of walking. Yet, we can also use this word together with an article in *a walk*, in which case it is a noun. In (b) *eat* is a verb, describing an action. Also *go* (c) is a verb in the example *I go*, while *I would like to have a go* would be a noun. In (d), *like* would be a verb in an example such as *I like him*, as it describes a state. Yet some speakers also talk about *a like on Facebook*, in which case *like* is a noun. *Room* (e) is a typical noun as in *a room*, yet it could also be used verbally in examples such as *can we room together?*[12] *Generate* (f) is a verb, as is *employ* in (g). Also *do* in (h) appears as a typical verb at first, but this form can also be used nominally in some varieties of English, referring to a party, as in *it was a great do*. *Overdo* (h), on the other hand, can only be used as a verb.

4.6 ADJECTIVES

Adjectives tell us what something is like, giving nuances; they turn *the cake* into *the **tasty** cake*, and *a story* into *an **exciting** story*. The two adjectives shown here, *tasty* and *exciting*, appear in noun phrases, which means they appear after an article (*the* or *a*) and tell us more about the type of *cake* or *story* with which we are dealing. Linguists tend to call this 'modification', i.e. the adjectives modify the nouns with which they appear.

There is also another way in which adjectives can occur, together with a type of verb called a *copular verb* such as *is*, *seems*, *appears*, *looks*, *becomes* and the like. Copular verbs can be described as similar to =, the "equals" sign. These verbs are often used when the speaker wants to highlight a specific feature, for example *the cake looks tasty* is quite similar to the example above, but rather than appearing hidden away in a noun phrase 'the ... cake', the adjective *tasty* is focused, appearing on its own after the copular verb *look*.

4.7 ADVERBS

Adverbs are in many ways very similar to adjectives. While adjectives describe the properties of nouns, adverbs tell us more about verbs. This includes concepts such as the time, place or manner in which something happens (*yesterday*, *here* and *slowly*). In English there are two types of adverbs: those that derive from adjectives through the addition on -*ly* and those that do not. Our example *slowly* describes an action, such as *he drives slowly*. Yet, without the adverb marker -*ly* it is used as an adjective, as in *the slow car*. We could put together a full list of those adverbs that do not have adjectival counterparts. These adverbs typically give information about time, place and manner, and include words like *tomorrow* and *here*. Yet, also converted words such as *home* (see the example above) can function as adverbs in certain environments. Crucially, these forms are adverbs when they describe the manner of the verbal action, the time or place of the action in more detail.

4.8 PRONOUNS

The name of this word class gives an indication of the functions of *pronouns*: they appear *pro* 'for, on behalf of' *nouns*. In this way, *personal pronouns* such as *he* can appear instead of noun phrases such as *Jim* or *the man*. English personal pronouns include *I, you, he, she, it, we, you* and *they, me, him, her, us, them*.

Demonstrative pronouns are those used to 'demonstrate' or point at things such as *this, that, these* and *those*. *Reflexive pronouns* such as *yourself, myself, themselves*, and so on, which refer back to a person introduced elsewhere in a clause.[13] *Possessive pronouns* indicate ownership, such as *my, his, her, our, your* and *their*. *Interrogative pronouns* are used in questions, such as *why, who, what* and *when*. These are also sometimes referred to as *wh-words*; can you guess why? Incidentally, the exception *how* is also an interrogative pronoun and wh-word. There are other types of pronouns, such as relative pronouns, which we will look at briefly in chapter 6 about sentence structures.

4.9 PARTICLES AND OTHER WORD CLASSES

If you ask a linguist how many word classes a given language has, the answer may well be 'I don't know' or 'it depends'. This is usually because it really depends on how you divide up the word classes at the fringes, those small classes of elements that do not belong to the big groups of nouns, verbs and adjectives.[14] Sometimes these 'other' word classes are summarized under the heading of *particles*. Yet, there are clear differences in the functions of some of these.

One word class sometimes treated under the general heading of 'particles' are definite and indefinite articles, which we saw in conjunction with noun phrases above. Indeed, appearing with noun phrases is the typical function of these elements. But in some cases, demonstrative pronouns may take their place, such as in *that house*. Also, the indefinite article is restricted to single (*singular*) nouns, while in the *plural* indefinite nouns appear without an article: we say *the houses* but not **a houses*. Likewise, some nouns that refer to uncountable entities, also called *mass nouns*, appear without articles, e.g. *water* refers to the substance, not the (countable) quantity. When we say *the water* or even *a water*, we usually refer to a specific (implied) quantity, such as *a glass of water*, which is countable and therefore a *count noun*. Finally, not all languages have articles. In Mosetén (an Amazonian language from Bolivia), 'house' is *aka´*, which also means 'the house' and 'a house'.

Prepositions are another small group of words that are sometimes treated as particles. They are generally used to position something in time and place, and include *in, between, over, behind* and *before*. They are called prepositions because they generally appear before 'pre' the noun phrase they 'position', such as *to the house, before the big day, between us*. Some other languages have postpositions, putting the word after 'post' the noun phrase.

Conjunctions are used to put sentences together. In English, these are separate words such as *or, while* and *because*. There are two types. Conjunctions of the first type combine sentences or other words (noun phrases, verbs, adjectives) at the same level. These are called coordinating conjunctions, which in English are *and, or* and *but*:

(18) *Will you **leave or play?***
(19) ***John and Mary.***
(20) *A **tangy but nice** orange.*

The other type of conjunctions are *subordinating conjunctions*. They connect two sentences in such a way that one is additional, 'subordinated', to the other. We will briefly look at such subordinations in chapter 6.

Sometimes treated under the heading of particles are *quantifiers* of the type *many, few, all, every* and so on.

Other typical particles include *discourse markers*, such as *uhm, well, yeah*, which in itself is a rather large class of items with different functions. Some of these are present in the written language, such as *tag questions* isn't it? or *right?*, while others rarely appear in written form, such as the filler *uhm*, which is generally used by speakers to gain time for processing.

4.10 A WORD OF CAUTION

From this overview, you will have seen that there are a number of ways to define word classes in English and other languages. Still, it is difficult to look at word classes in isolation. We had to refer to verbs, adjectives and articles when defining nouns. We looked at noun phrases when distinguishing different types of verbs in terms of their transitivity, and so on. Also, we saw that some words such as *home* can be used in a range of different ways. If we look up *home* in isolation in a dictionary, we may be given the word class 'noun', as this is its main function. If it is a good dictionary, we will be presented with examples of the word used in different contexts and word classes, which in turn can help us establish to which class our word belongs. Yet, it is not enough to just look up words in a dictionary, to find out which word class they belong to, and we may be led astray that way. It is always important to look at a word in the environment it is used. One way to do so is to analyse the grammar with which the word appears, which is the topic of chapter 5.

4.11 WORD CLASSES IN THE LANGUAGES OF THE WORLD

When we discussed the different word classes above, we looked mainly at English. Even in one single language like English, it can be difficult to establish how many separate word classes there are, and not even linguists can reach a consensus. Looking at other languages across the globe, there are striking similarities, yet also differences in the way words are divided into classes and the ways in which linguists relate to these classes.

Many familiar languages distinguish between nouns, verbs and adjectives, yet there are nonetheless languages where this is not the case. In English and most other European languages, adjectives belong to an open class, which means that there are many adjectives and new items can be added to the class of adjectives at any one time. Yet, in some languages, such as the Nigerian language Igbo, adjectives belong to a closed class of very few items. Velupillai (2012: 128) also shows that some languages do not have adjectives at all. Many of these languages are indigenous languages of North and South America, as well as Australia. Again, the concepts expressed by adjectives can be expressed in other ways. For example in Hausa, *he is kind* is expressed as *he is with kindness*, in this case using a noun. (Velupillai 2012; Schachter & Shopen 2007).

Some other languages, such as the Riau variety of Indonesian, it is claimed, show no distinction between nouns and verbs. In this way, Gil (2013) argues convincingly that words expressing things (prototypical nouns) and activities (prototypical verbs) are treated in the same way and appear in the same grammatical environments.

There are other weird and wonderful examples of how languages can organize their grammars. For example, in the Australian indigenous language Iwaidja, kinship relationships are expressed through verbs (Evans 2000). In this way the English *father* is expressed as the equivalent of verbs meaning *to be father to, to have a father* and *to consider a father*, among others. Another curious example is the case of two words equivalent to the English conjunction 'and' in Walman, a language from Papua New Guinea. These are expressed as verbs (Brown & Dryer 2008), in that they show verbal inflectional forms (see chapter 5, where I will be discussing the grammar of words in more detail).

FURTHER READING

If you want to read more about words and word classes, you have a big choice in available materials. Again, you can choose between books as well as online resources. For example, there is a wealth of teaching resources on word classes, most of which is available for free online. Additionally, I have put together a number of videos about word classes, such as prepositions, which you can find by searching for 'Jeanette Sakel videos'.

While many books treat word classes, not many are devoted to this topic alone. Usually word classes are treated together with other topics, such as morphology, teaching English, grammar, typology and so on. Good overviews of word classes and their grammar that complements the introduction in the present book can be found in the first chapter of Tallerman's (2014) *Understanding syntax*, 4th edition; chapter 6 of Velupillai's (2012) *Linguistic typology*; and chapter 2 of Moravcsik's (2012) *Language typology*. These chapters also include more information about transitivity.

If you are interested in languages with less clearly defined word classes, you can have a look at a book devoted to this topic: Rijkhoff & van Lier's (2013) *Flexible word classes*. While this edited volume is predominantly written for an academic audience, you may be able to look for specific examples of languages in which word class divisions are less rigidly defined (see also chapter 11 for a few tips on how to read difficult texts).

If you would like to read more about lexicology and lexicography, including the way dictionaries are put together, I recommend Halliday & Yallop (2007) *Lexicology – a short introduction* and *The Oxford guide to practical lexicography* by Atkins and Rundell (2008).

If you are interested in how many words you know in a language, such as English, you can try to find _vocabulary_ tests to investigate your level of knowledge. Searching for 'vocabulary test' will give you a number of online options, where based on questionnaires your overall vocabulary knowledge will be calculated.

NOTES

1   All three of these words are acronyms. *Laser* stands for *Light Amplification by Stimulated Emission of Radiation. Radar* stands for *RAdio Detection And Ranging. Dvd* stands for *Digital Versatile Disc.* In each case the capital letters together form the acronym.

2   The definition of *selfie* is 'a picture one has taken of oneself', e.g. with a smartphone.

3   If you delve deeper into linguistics, you may come across languages that have only a subset of these. Some languages have even been argued not to distinguish any of these categories.

4   This does not mean that new forms never make it to these categories, but they are much more difficult and generally take longer to be integrated. Usually there is another good reason for the introduction of a new preposition, such as contact with a language that has such a form.

5   Having said this, most European languages like German have thousands of nouns and far fewer other items. So this method can still be quite effective! Also, knowing *Badezimmer* 'bathroom', my friend could easily deduce the verb *baden* 'to bath' and thereby learn a verb.

6   A sub-grouping of concrete nouns are _proper nouns_, which are essentially names referring to individual people, beings or places.

7   Recall from above that noun phrases can consist of one word like *Peter* or *she*, or they can contain more elements referring to the same nominal entity, such as *the ginger **cat*** or *our **car**, which had just been repaired.*

8   We also talk about noun phrases when there is just a single noun without any additional articles or other elements.

9   Many linguists consider ditransitive verbs a subclass of transitive verbs.

10   Note that some linguists avoid the term *verb phrase* because of its theoretical implications. For example, this term was deliberately left out of the 2014 glossary of grammatical terminology for schools (by Dick Hudson and colleagues http://www.lagb-education.org/grammatical-terminology-for-schools). I use it here merely to express 'the verb and the other elements immediately associated with the verb', such as auxiliaries.

11   Indeed, the verb *hit* can have two separate functions: it can express actions in the 'now' *These days I never hit the target*, as well as in the 'past' *I hit all the targets last year.*

12   This type of verbal use of *room* may be restricted to certain varieties of English. There are also other verbal uses of *to room*, for example to express 'to have space for'.

13   Take, for example *He sees himself in the mirror*, where *he* is the subject of the clause and *himself* is the object of the clause, marked this way to indicate that it is the same person as the subject. Compare this to *He sees him in the mirror*, in which case *him* would most likely be interpreted to be a different person from *he*.

14   Some linguists even discuss whether nouns, verbs and adjectives exist in some languages. Thus, the word classes are far from straightforward.

The grammar of words

IN THIS CHAPTER

In this chapter, I move beyond individual words and word classes, and look at the grammar with which words appear. I will introduce the study of morphology, defining morphemes as the smallest meaningful units in language. I will then move on to different grammatical categories of nouns, verbs and adjectives, introducing the concepts of inflection and derivation. This chapter contains:

- Morphemes

- Affixes: suffixes, prefixes and infixes

- Derivation and inflection

- Nominal inflectional categories: case, number, person, gender

- Verbal inflectional categories: tense, aspect, mood

- Agreement.

5.1 MORPHEMES

In the previous chapter we divided words into word classes according to their meaning, the context in which they are used and the function of the elements with which they appear. For example, English nouns can appear with the definite article *the*. We also saw that words can combine more than one meaning, as in *cherrytree*, a compound of *cherry* and *tree*. Let us now consider *cherrytrees*, which is even more complex. It combines three meanings: *cherry, tree* and *–s*. This last element *–s* indicates the plural, which means it tells us that we are talking about more than one *cherrytree*. Each of these three elements has a specific meaning, yet they are not all words. While you may agree that *cherry* and *tree* are words in their own right, *–s* cannot really appear on its own meaning 'more than one'. It has to be added to another word, which is why I have written it with a little dash at the front (the place where it needs to attach to another word). The meaning of *–s* is purely grammatical: it simply adds information about number, in this case more than one.

> ### Exercise 5.1
>
> The single letter –*s* in the example above has a clear meaning. Do you think we can find meanings in each letter of *cherry*? Which meaning does *c* have, or *ch*?

So, *cherry* cannot be divided up any further, as the different parts of *cherry* do not have a specific meaning. It is, in a way, 'the smallest meaningful unit'. The same is the case for *tree. Cherry, tree* and –*s* are the smallest meaningful units we can find. We call these _morphemes_.

Morphemes constitute a way to divide words up according to the different elements that have specific meanings. Another way that you may be more familiar with is the division of words into rhythmic units, namely _syllables_. Our example *cherrytrees* would be divided up quite differently in this case, into *che-rry-trees* (see chapter 3). While the division into rhythmic units is important in poetry, music and phonology, it does not tell us much about the overall grammatical forms (and functions) of the different word-parts. Hence, when dividing words up for the analysis of grammar, we look at morphemes rather than syllables.

When looking at the grammar of words, morphemes are important, which is why I will explore them in a little more detail here. They are also important in our discussion of grammatical elements, such as *tense* and *person*, which we will look at more closely later on in this chapter.[1]

5.2 DIFFERENT TYPES OF MORPHEMES

We saw that *cherry-tree-s* consists of three morphemes, which can be presented with dashes to indicate where the morpheme boundaries fall. Two of these morphemes are words in their own right: *cherry* and *tree* can both appear on their own, they are _free morphemes_. The plural marker –*s*, on the other hand, has to be attached to another morpheme, it is a _bound morpheme_.

Bound morphemes can appear in various places. In the case of –*s*, it was added to the end of the word *cherrytree*. A bound morpheme that appears at the *end* is called a _suffix_. Bound morphemes can also appear elsewhere: In the word *un-real* the bound morpheme *un-* appears before the free element *real*. In this case, *un-* is a _prefix_ (note that the dash appears after the *un-*, as it is added before the element it attaches to). There are further _affixes_, the cover term for prefixes and suffixes in English, such as infixes in slang: *fan-bleedin-tastic* consists of the word *fantastic*, which has been changed by the addition of an _infix_ -*bleedin-*.[2] Infixes are quite rare in English, and typically appear in slang. In some other languages, however, infixes are used for regular grammatical categories, such as repeated actions.[3]

Apart from looking at the places where morphemes occur, we can also divide morphemes into types according to their function. Bound morphemes, as discussed here, can have different functions.

Exercise 5.2

Before you read on, try to do the following exercise. You are presented with words (*fair*, *house* and *walk*) and examples of bound morphemes with which they appear. For each bound morpheme, describe in your own words what it adds to the overall meaning or function of the word. Once you have done that, try to establish which word class (or word classes) each of the examples belongs to:

    a   *fair, un-fair, fair-ness, fair-er*
    b   *house, house-s, house's*
    c   *walk, walk-ed, walk-s*

Let us begin with *fair* and the affixes it occurs with in this exercise. The form *un-* expresses the opposite meaning, *-ness* indicates the concept of being *fair*, and *-er* relates *fair* to the overall context, indicating that in this case something is *more fair* than something else. The word *fair* on its own is an adjective, as are *unfair* and *fairer*, while *fairness* is a noun. It can, for example, appear with a definite article *the fairness (of it all)*. In this way, the word class has been changed, as has its overall meaning. While the word class is not changed in the case of *unfair*, which remains an adjective, the meaning certainly has changed completely. In the case of *fairer*, the word class and overall meaning remain the same as in *fair*, and the only difference is that *fairer* relates to the context in which *fair* is used in comparison to something else.

There are two different processes involved in the affixes appearing with *fair*. In the first case, the meaning of the word is changed, as in *fairness* and *unfair* and we talk about *derivation*. When the meaning remains the same and only the context in which the word is used changes, as in *fairer*, we talk about *inflection*. We will explore these definitions in some more detail below.

Let us look at the other examples in the exercise above in terms of derivation and inflection. *House* can be classified as a noun as it can appear with a definite article, as in *the house*. Yet, as we saw in the previous chapter, it can also be used verbally, as in *we house several dogs at the moment*. If we came across the written word form *house-s*, in isolation then, we could interpret it as either a noun in the plural (*two houses*) or as a verb in the third person singular (*he house-s several dogs*). There are, thus, two suffixes of the form *–s*, indicating either 'plurality' in nouns or appearing with verb marking that the subject is a *third person singular* (*he, she, it, John, Mary, that guy*, etc., see the discussion below in this chapter). Which one of these suffixes is used depends, again, on the context in which the word *house* is used. Thus, we always have to consider the context in which a word is used in order to understand which word class it belongs to, and to establish the meaning of the affixes appearing with the word. In the case of *house-'s*, that is a bit easier, as this form can only be used as a noun. The *-'s* indicates that something belongs, or relates, to the house, such as *the house-'s roof*. Notice here that you could also have chosen to say *the roof of the house*, another way to express such belonging or relationships, so English has two ways of expressing possession. With human possessors, the possessive –*s* is often favoured, such as *John's cat* (versus *the cat of John*).

The final examples, *walk*, *walk-ed*, *walk-s* are, in many ways, similar to *house*. While *walk* can be classified as a verb, as it expresses an inherent action, it could also be a noun, as in *the walk*. The form *walk-ed*, then, is *walk* in the *past tense*, and can only be a verb, as there is no nominal form that looks like this. *Walk-s*, however, is again dependent on the context it appears in. If it is used as a verb, as in *she walks*, the –*s* suffix tells us that the subject is a third person singular. If it is a noun, like in *the walk-s*, the –*s* indicates the plural.

What do you think: are we dealing with inflection (the basic meaning remains the same) or derivation (the meaning changes) in the examples of *house* and *walk* above? When we look at the nominal uses of *house* and their meaning, they all refer to *house* used in different grammatical contexts, such as 'more than one house' and 'belonging to the house', without changing the core meaning of *house* itself. When we look at the verbal uses of *walk*, they all refer to the same action, just in different contexts of time (past tense) and the person carrying out the action (a third person singular). They would, thus, all be analysed as inflection.

To summarize this section, there are two different types of affixes: those that change the inherent meaning of the word (as *un-* in *un-fair*) and those that retain the core meaning, but put the word into a different context (such as the past tense marker –*ed* in *walk-ed*). We call the first of these affixes derivational affixes, and the second type inflectional affixes. I'll now discuss derivation and inflection in some more detail.

5.3 DERIVATION

Derivation is a way to form new words by changing the inherent meaning of a word. You can think of derivation as a way to form new entries in a dictionary. Words affected by derivation can retain their original word class, as the adjectives *fair* and its opposite *unfair*. Yet, if you notice a change in word class, you are definitely dealing with derivation. Thus, *fair* is an adjective, while *fairness* is a noun. By adding the suffix –*ness* to an adjective X, we can form nouns meaning something like 'the state of being X'. Yet, we also saw that a word class can change by using a word in a different context, such as *I walk* (verb) and *a walk* (noun). This process of conversion (see chapter 4) could be considered a special case of derivation, without an affix.[4]

5.4 INFLECTION

When it comes to grammar, inflection tends to be the place of action. In this case, no new words are formed. Rather, the old word meanings remain, but they are put into a new, we may say 'grammatical', context. Thus, *walk* and *walked* are the same verb, which we could look up in a dictionary under the same entry. What is different is the grammatical context: *walk* is used in the *present tense*, *walked* is past tense. Inflectional categories in nouns include categories such as *number, person, case* and *gender*. Typical verbal categories are tense, aspect, mood and *modality*. Adjectives can inflect for *comparison*. I will go through these typical types of inflection in the following sections.

5.4.1 Inflection of nouns and other nominal forms

Nominal inflection is sometimes referred to as *declension*, especially in traditional grammar books and materials aimed at learners of a second language. The term declension may cover adjectival inflection as well.[5] In linguistics, however, this term is rarely used and we tend to refer to it as (nominal) inflection.

English nouns inflect for number. Thus, we have a singular form of a noun *house*, and a plural form *house-s*, in which the suffix *-s* is the inflectional marker indicating the plural. Most plurals in English are formed this way, but there are also some notable exceptions, such as *children, oxen, sheep, antennae, phenomena* and more. These are *irregular* plural forms.

Exercise 5.3

Look up the above irregular forms in a dictionary and try to determine why these forms look different from those ending in *–s*. Consider whether you have ever used or witnessed others use forms such as *childs, oxes, sheeps, antennas* or *phenomenons* (or, incidentally, *phenomena* in the singular, such as in *this is a new phenomena*)? Who would use these forms, and why? You may add your own examples of exceptional plural forms to this list.

There are two main reasons for exceptional plural forms in English. The first one is that forms like *children, sheep* and *oxen* are historical remnants of an older form of English. The other forms are loanwords, usually from Latin and Greek, which were borrowed together with their singular and plural forms. That means the irregular forms are actually inflectional forms from another language! Sometimes you hear children and non-native speakers use forms such as *childs* or *sheeps* that a native English speaker may not find acceptable. Yet, even native English speakers can be heard talking about *oxes* and *antennas*. The reason is that speakers 'regularize' the irregular forms. A reason can be that the speakers do not use these words very often and were not conscious of the irregular forms at the time of speaking. *Phenomena* is an interesting case, as many native English speakers now use the original plural form *phenomena* to refer to singular and plural occurrences. I have, on occasion, also heard the regularized form *phenomenas* being used. One plural form that has become fixed and *regular* as a singular is *agenda*, which appears with the regular plural *agendas* even in highly formal speech.

While English nouns inflect for number, other languages have more inflectional categories appearing with nouns. Yet, even English has further nominal categories, but these only show up in pronouns. English pronouns can be *marked* for number, person, gender and case. We will explore case in more detail in the following chapter 6 on sentences, and concentrate on number, gender and person here. Have a look at the following *paradigm*, which is a way of representing these forms in a table for a better overview. I have merged the cells in the table that are overlapping, showing how the second person is the same in the singular and plural, and how there is a gender distinction in the third person singular, but not in the plural:

Table 5.1
English personal pronouns

	singular		plural
1st person	I̲		w̲e̲
2nd person		y̲o̲u̲	
3rd person masculine	h̲e̲		
3rd person feminine	s̲h̲e̲		t̲h̲e̲y̲
3rd person neuter	i̲t̲		

Exercise 5.4

I would like you to look at the inflectional categories of English pronouns. Try to establish, for each form, the categories for which the pronouns inflect. For example: *he* inflects for three categories: person (3rd person), number (singular) and gender (*masculine*). Since another person (say, 2nd person) is marked differently *you*, plural is marked differently *they* and the other gender (*feminine*) is marked differently *she*.

Now over to you: what are the inflectional categories for *I*, *we*, *she*, *you*, *it*, *they*? [hint: not all inflect for all three categories]

When looking through the forms, you will find that *I* merely marks for person (1st person) and number (singular) but not gender, as it can be used by feminine and masculine speakers. *We*, likewise, inflects for person (1st person) and number (plural) but not gender. *She* marks for person (3rd person), number (singular) and gender (feminine). *You* inflects for person (2nd person) but not number (it can be used in the singular and the plural), nor gender. *It* inflects for person (3rd person), number (singular) and gender (*neuter*). Finally, *they* marks for person (3rd person), number (plural) but not gender.

Thus, we only have gender marking in the third person singular. When you think about it, *gender* is a curious category. You may understand the use of gender in pronouns, referring to the sex of a person or animal. Yet, why do languages such as German use feminine, masculine and neuter for all nouns in the language? What makes *das Boot* 'the boat' neuter, *die Sonne* 'the sun' feminine and *der Stern* 'the star' masculine? While many gender systems have a semantic core, this may not always be obvious to the speakers of the language. In some cases, gender system divide up nouns according to their *animacy* (whether they are human, animate as in animals or plants or inanimate, for example), in others gender depends on the morphological forms of words (for example words ending in -*a* are classed as feminine). In other languages the shape or size of objects determines the gender to which they belong. In this case the term *noun class* is sometimes used rather than gender.

5.4.2 Nominal agreement

Nominal categories such as gender and number tend to be marked on other words than just nouns. For example, definite articles (or other such *determiners* in a noun phrase) and adjectives (and other *modifiers*) in Portuguese show *agreement* with the nouns with which they appear. That means they mark for the gender and number of that noun, thereby *agreeing* in these categories with the noun. In example (21a), the noun *coisa* 'thing' is feminine and singular, and triggers feminine singular agreement in the definite article *a* 'the' and the adjective *pequena* 'small'. In (21b) *coisa-s* is in the plural. In this case, the definite article and the adjective agree with the feminine and plural categories. Examples with a masculine noun *menino* 'boy' are given for comparison in (22):

(21a) *a*   *coisa*   *pequen-a*
       the.F(SG)[6]   thing(F)(SG)   small-F(SG)
       'the small thing'

(21b) *a-s*   *coisa-s*   *pequen-a-s*
       the.F-PL   thing(F)-PL   small-F-PL
       'the small things'

(22a) *o*   *menino*   *pequen-o*
       the.M(SG)   boy(M)(SG)   small-M(SG)
       'the small boy'

(22b) *o-s*   *menino-s*   *pequen-o-s*
       the.M-PL   boy(M)-PL   small-M-PL
       'the small boys'

Note the way linguistic examples are represented: the first line shows the example in the language, with morphemes separated by dashes (-). The second line is what we call a *gloss*, that is a word-by-word translation indicating the gender (F = feminine, M = masculine) and number (PL = plural). Note that (SG) means the number is part of the word form, while -F means that there is a separable suffix indicating that the word is feminine. The final line of each example gives the overall translation.

English has less agreement of this kind in the noun phrase, yet we can find examples of demonstrative pronouns agreeing in number with the noun. For example, *this house* in the singular appears with the singular demonstrative pronoun *this*, while *these houses* in the plural appears with the plural demonstrative pronoun *these*.

5.4.3 Inflection of adjectives

Note how in the last section the adjective was marked for the gender and number of the noun with which it appeared. This is a form of inflection we called agreement. Yet, there is another way in which adjectives can inflect without agreeing with the nouns with which they appear. This is through comparison, with the typical categories *comparative* and *superlative*. The comparative expresses that something is 'more' than something else, such as our example *fair-er* above. The superlative makes an element stand out as the highest degree in relation to others, such as *the fair-est*.

5.4.4 Inflection of verbs

In the same way as nouns inflect for categories, verbs can also be marked for the grammatical environments in which they appear. In some traditional grammars, verbal inflection is referred to as *conjugation*, yet, again, linguists tend to prefer the term verbal inflection.

In chapter 5 we briefly mentioned auxiliary verbs marking the categories of tense, aspect and mood/modality. Auxiliaries commonly mark these categories, at least in languages such as English and other European languages. Still, English tense marking can also be done through suffixation. The past tense and present tense are marked in this way, such as in the examples with *walk* discussed above: *I walk, he walk-s, he walk-ed*. The past tense is marked by *-ed* in the entire verbal paradigm, while the present tense remains *unmarked* (that means, there is no suffix on the verb) in all persons and numbers other than the third person singular (*he walk-s*). This differs from *he walk-ed*, which is the same form as *I walk-ed*; this means that the third person singular marker *–s* is, indeed, a marker restricted to the present tense.[7]

In the cases where tense, aspect and mood are marked by auxiliary verbs, these occur with so-called *participles*. English has present and past participles:

(23) *She is **walking** = present participle.*
(24) *She has **walked** = past participle.*

You will probably be familiar with the present participle as the *-ing* form in English, while the past participle in (24) is the same as the past tense form of the verb (*she walked*). Yet, there are also irregular verbs for which the past participle is different from the past tense form, for example in the verb *eat*:

(25) *He has **eaten** = past participle.*
(26) *He **ate** = past tense.*

Exceptions prove the rule, it is said, and this is generally the case with all inflections. When learning a language, you may come across irregular verbs. In English the past tense is often expressed by the morpheme *-ed* added to the verb form. Thus, *walk* becomes *walk-ed* in the past tense. The same form is used in the past participle, such as in *I have walked*, where *walked* is the past participle. A large number of verbs do this, and we can refer to the *-ed* forms as the regular past tense (and past participle) forms in English. Yet, there are also some irregular verbs that do not. For example *eat* does not have the past tense for **eated*, but rather *ate*. It also has a different past participle form, which is *eaten*, as in *I eat* (present tense), *I ate* (past tense) and *I have eaten* (perfect aspect – using the past participle form).

French and Spanish, have different *verb classes* (some people call these conjugations), which often present different *infinitive* forms, and also tend to differ across the inflectional forms. For example, Spanish verbs for which the infinitive form ends in *-er* have different inflectional forms from those verbs for which the infinitives end in *-ar* and *-ir*.

In English the infinitive sometimes appears with the infinitive marker *to*, such as *to go*. The infinitive is a curious category that exists in European languages, but is less frequent across the languages of the world. In those languages that have it, the infinitive tends to be the form we find in a dictionary. In Spanish, *caminar* 'to walk' is the infinitive of the verb that appears in a dictionary, as opposed to the inflectional forms 1SG *camino*, 2SG *caminas*, and so on. Infinitives sometimes appear in certain constructions, which in English include the marking of mood (see below) and specific types of *subordinate clauses* (see chapter 6).

5.4.5 Tense and aspect

Tense and aspect overlap to a great deal in English and other languages, which is why I have decided to treat them together in this section.

Tense, we saw in the examples above, refers to the time of an action or event. It can be present tense (27a) at the 'now'. The past tense (27b) is the time 'before now', or the *future tense* (27c) is 'after now':

(27a)   *He bakes a cake.*
(27b)   *He baked a cake.*
(27c)   *He will bake a cake.*

Aspect refers to the way an event is built up internally. For example, an event can be classified as ongoing (28), using the *progressive* aspect.

(28)   *He is baking a cake.*

We could also focus on the result or completion of an action or event, referred to as *perfect* aspect, as in (29):

(29)   *He has eaten the doughnut.*

As a matter of fact, tense and aspect can occur together. While the example of the perfect aspect in (29) is in the present tense, the perfect aspect can appear in the past tense (30) and future tense (31):

(30)   *He had eaten the doughnut.*
(31)   *He will have eaten the doughnut.*

In the case of the perfect aspect, the focus is on the endpoint of the event, independent of whether that endpoint is in the past, present or future.

The perfect and progressive aspects are marked in English by the combination of auxiliaries and participles. In this way, the auxiliary *have* and the past participle form the perfect aspect, while the progressive aspect is marked by the auxiliary *be* and the present participle. Other languages distinguish further types of aspect, such as the *iterative*, which means 'repeated', as in *clap your hands (repeatedly)*; *inceptive*, which means 'beginning', focusing on the start of an action, as in *she started to paint*; *punctual*, referring to a single occasion of an event, as in *he sneezed*, and *habitual* referring to something happening again and again, as in *the girl reads books*.

Because tense and aspect are often linked in languages, there is a wealth of terminology used to refer to these categories. You may have heard about the *pluperfect*, which really is the combination of the past tense ('before now') with the perfect aspect ('focus on the completed action'), as in He **had locked** *the door (when she came back)*. Likewise, the 'present continuous' is the combination of the present tense ('now') with the progressive aspect ('an ongoing action'), as in *She **is dancing**. Some languages will use very specific and often confusing terminology. For example the term *preterite* can be used for different tense and aspect combinations. Most often it combines the past tense with an aspectual form (sometimes referred to as the 'perfective') that indicates that events were completed in the past.

5.4.6 Mood and modality

Modality refers to the attitudes or beliefs a speaker expresses when describing an action. In some languages, this is part of the verbal inflectional system, which is referred to as mood. In English, modality is mainly expressed through auxiliaries. Yet, since languages differ in the ways in which they express these categories (and since these overlap), mood and modality are usually treated under the same heading.

Exercise 5.5

What, do you think, is the attitude of the speaker in each of the following examples? The parts of the clause that indicate the mood are in bold print. Even if you do not know the term for it, try to explain what the speaker wants to express:

a   *You **should leave**.*
b   *You **ought to leave**.*
c   *You **may leave**.*
d   ***Leave!***
e   *If you **would leave** (I could go to sleep).*
f   *I suggest you **leave**. [see also: I suggest he leave.]*
g   *You **leave**.*

In (a) and (b) the auxiliaries *should* and *ought* are used together with the infinitive *(to) leave* to indicate an obligation, or rather to reveal the speaker's attitude that 'you' have an obligation to leave. In (c), the speaker allows 'you' to leave. Yet, this could also be understood as a polite request to leave. In (d) the request is not hidden by politeness. This is a so-called *imperative*, which is basically an order. In English, imperatives appear without personal pronouns, and in this case 'you' is understood. Example (e) expresses an outcome under a certain condition, also referred to as the *conditional*. Example (f) gives a remnant of a structure that has all but disappeared from English, called the *subjunctive*. It can be used to express wishes, opinions or specific requirements. Note that in the third person singular example given in brackets the verb is *leave* and not *leaves*, i.e. the inflectional form for the third person singular does not appear in the subjunctive.[8] Some Romance languages, like Spanish, make frequent use of the subjunctive when referring to actions or events that have so far not come true. The final example (g) does not express any specific mood as such, but rather shows the unmarked form. In the study of mood and modality, linguists refer to this basic form as the *indicative*.

Just like tense and aspect, mood can be marked by suffixes or through auxiliary verbs. English indicates mood using 'modal auxiliaries' followed by infinitives (in examples a, b, c and e).

Exercise 5.6

Compare the following verb phrases: how do the meanings differ? Indicate which tense, aspect and mood is used in each case:

I have eaten, I had eaten, I will eat, I am eating, I should eat, I would eat, Will I eat?

I have eaten indicates that an event is completed (perfect) in the present tense 'now'. *I had eaten*, on the other hand, is the perfect in the past tense. *I will eat* indicates the future tense with no indication of the internal structure of the event, that is no marking for aspect. *I am eating* is in the present tense and progressive aspect. *I should eat* indicates an obligation through the use of the modal auxiliary *should* in the present tense. *I would eat* also makes use of a modal auxiliary but in this case indicates the possibility or even likelihood of eating, again in the present tense. *Will I eat?* is a question in the future tense. Notice that in this example the pronoun *I* and the auxiliary *will* are switched around, a process referred to as *inversion*. We will come back to inversion when we discuss questions in chapter 6.

5.5 AGREEMENT IN THE CLAUSE

We saw that nominal inflectional categories such as gender and number can appear on definite articles and adjectives that appear together with the noun. Such agreement is also possible with verbs. Consider the following examples from English:

(32a)   *I walk*
(32b)   *She walk-s*

As we saw above, an English verb is marked by *-s*, as in *walk-s*, when the noun it appears with (its <u>subject</u>, to be discussed in chapter 6) is in the third person singular and the verb is in the present tense. In the third person plural *they walk*, there is no marking by *-s*. Furthermore, this marking only appears in the present tense. In the past tense *she walked* receives no additional marking by *-s*. There are even further exceptions. Some verbs do not show agreement at all, such as modal auxiliaries like *he can, I can*. Finally, the verb *be* appears with more fine-grained inflectional forms, outlined in the following paradigm, given next to *walk* to show the difference:

Table 5.2
The English verbal paradigm

Singular		Present Tense		Past Tense	
1st person	I	am	/walk	was	/walked
2nd person	you	are	/walk	were	/walked
3rd person	she	is	/walks	was	/walked
Plural					
1st person	we	are	/walk	were	/walked
2nd person	you	are	/walk	were	/walked
3rd person	they	are	/walk	were	/walked

Exercise 5.7

Take a look at the forms of the auxiliary and copular verb *be* in the paradigm above and compare them to the forms of *walk*. Where does *be* differ? Which inflectional categories are marked in *be*?

We can see that in the present tense the verb *be* also marks for the first person singular *am*, while this form is not marked in other verbs, such as *walk* in the example. In the past tense, *be* again distinguishes between the first and third person singular and the rest of the forms. This time the forms for the first and third person singular are the same, *was*, while the remaining forms are *were*.

Agreement can give us an indication of the subject with which a verb appears. While this is quite restricted in English, other languages such as European Spanish have much more elaborate agreement systems. Each verb form has a special ending depending on the person (1st, 2nd, 3rd) and number (singular, plural) with which it appears.

Exercise 5.8

Compare the following Spanish verbal paradigm for *caminar* 'to walk' with the English paradigms for *be* and *walk* above, and indicate for each form the categories with which the verb agrees. For example, *camino* reflects the number (singular) and person (1st person) of the subject it occurs with:[9]

Table 5.3
The Spanish verbal paradigm

Singular		Present Tense	Past Tense
1st person	(yo)	camino	caminé
2nd person	(tu)	caminas	caminaste
3rd person	(ella)[1]	camina	caminó
Plural			
1st person	(nosotras)	caminamos	caminamos
2nd person	(vosotras)	camináis	caminasteis
3rd person	(ellas)	caminan	caminaron

Note
1 This is just one of the 3rd person singular forms, meaning 'she'. The same applies to the plural forms given in the paradigm, where I just give the feminine forms *vosotras* (2nd person plural F) and *ellas* (3rd person plural F) to illustrate the example.

You will see that in Spanish all forms mark for the person and number of the underlying subject noun phrase with which they appear. The difference in tense (present and past tense) is upheld in all persons other than the first person plural, for which the forms are the same.[10]

You may have noticed that the personal pronouns *I, you*, etc. were given without brackets in the English paradigm, but appear in brackets *(yo), (tu)*, and so on in the Spanish example. That is not a typo. Rather, while English verbs need to appear with a noun phrase to indicate who is doing what,[11] Spanish verbs can appear on their own without any further elements. We could say that one reason for why this is possible is that all verbs in Spanish indicate what their subject is in their verbal agreement forms, despite some minimal overlap between some forms (e.g. the first person plural present and past tense in our example above). In purely economical terms, Spanish does not 'need' to indicate what the subject of each verb is, as this is already given in the verbal ending.[12]

Some languages go even further and their verbs agree with both subject and *object*. This is, for example, the case in Mosetén:

(33) *Soba-kse-ja'*
      visit-3PL.OBJ-1PL.SUBJ
      'We visit them.'

In this case, *-kse-* refers to the object 'they' and *–ja'* refers to the subject 'we'.

The way in which subject and object interact, as well as a lot more to do with the structure of sentences will be discussed in the following chapter.

FURTHER READING

There are many good introductory morphology books, which treat the issues discussed in this chapter. Haspelmath and Sims (2010) *Understanding morphology* is a detailed introduction to the field with many exercises. Lieber (2010) *Introducing morphology* introduces words and morphological structures and has helpful advice on morphological analysis in English as well as other languages of the world. Books on linguistic typology deal with morphological categories across a wide range of languages, such as Velupillai (2012) *An introduction to linguistic typology* and Moravcsik (2012) *Introducing language typology.*

NOTES

1   When talking about 'words' linguists often prefer to call these *lexemes* rather than words. Lexemes are the abstract elements without grammatical information such as the plural *-s*. In that way, *cherrytree* and *cherrytrees* would be the same lexeme, we would look them up under the same entry in the dictionary.

2   In this case *-bleedin-* is not a bound morpheme, as it can appear on its own in slang, e.g. *this bleedin' dog*. We can argue that the few infixes used in English are all free morphemes.

3   An example of infixes is the *glottal stop* (written -'-) in Mosetén, which is used to express a repeated action, also referred to as an *iterative* action. Thus, *japits-* means 'put something in the mouth (to eat)', and with the infix *japi-'-ts-* means 'put something in the mouth repeatedly (e.g. eating fast)'.

4   Some linguists use the term zero-affix or Ø-affix to indicate that they would normally expect there to be a marker in this place, but that in this case the same phenomenon (derivation) happens without any formal marking.

5   This depends a lot on the language you are studying. In some languages, adjectives look much more like verbs, and a different terminology may be used.

6   Elements in brackets refer to features that are not overtly expressed by a morpheme, but understood in the context. In this case, *a* is feminine singular. The plural receives the morpheme *-s*, while there is no such morpheme in the singular (we can say it remains *unmarked*).

7   The phenomenon we encounter here, that one small suffix *-s* expresses three meanings in one, namely tense, person and number, is referred to as *fusion.*

8   From my experience very few speakers use the subjunctive, but would rather say *I suggest he leaves*, i.e. with the *-s* in place. In this case the subjunctive is replaced by the indicative form of the verb.

9   Observe that I only give the feminine forms of the personal pronouns where there are various forms to choose from. Also, the pronouns given here are European Spanish. The past tense forms given here refer to one of two past tense/aspectual distinctions in Spanish corresponding to the English past tense.

10 When forms in a paradigm are the same, such as the first person plural forms in the Spanish example, we call this *syncretism*.

11 Strictly speaking, there are a few exceptions, such as imperative clauses (commands) where the subject is left out or cases where the subject or object of a clause is understood in the speech context.

12 As always, not all languages work this way, and some languages, such as Mandarin Chinese, can have sentences that give little or no indication to the subject forms.

Clauses and sentences

IN THIS CHAPTER

This chapter explores the ways in which clauses and sentences are put together. You may wonder why I put both terms into the heading of this chapter, as they are often used interchangeably in English. Yet, linguists tend to prefer using 'clauses' to refer to simple clauses containing a subject and predicate (see below), while *sentences* are constructions consisting of more than one clause, such as complex sentences.

Many of the concepts we will explore in this chapter relate to the previous chapters on words and grammar, as well as the following chapter on semantics. The topics I will focus on in the current chapter are:

- Word order
- Phrases
- Subject and object
- Semantic roles
- Predicates
- Other syntactic structures: questions, negation, voice.

6.1 WORD ORDER

In most languages, words have to be arranged in a certain order, referred to as a language's *word order*. In English, we can say *Maya hugs Phoebe*, in which case Maya is the subject, the one 'doing something'. *Phoebe* is the *direct object*, the one that is being hugged. The verb[1] *hugs* appears between the subject and the direct object. In this basic English sentence, the word order is subject–verb–object, abbreviated *SVO* using the first letter of each term.

Should we conduct a more thorough investigation of clauses in English we would find that this is the *basic word order* of English. But there are other possible orders in the language. How about *Phoebe, Maya hugs, but she ignores Stanley*. In this example, a speaker would probably use a different intonation to make it clear that *Phoebe* the direct object of the clause receiving a special contrast. *Phoebe* appears at the front of the clause. This object–subject–verb (i.e. 'OSV') structure is a *marked word order*, meaning it is not the default, most frequent or basic way of making a statement. It only appears in cases where the direct object receives special focus, or in specific speech styles.

The *Star Wars* character Yoda is known to use this strategy in his speech, making statements such as *patience you must have*, where *patience* is the direct object and *you* is the subject of the clause. Yet, while Yoda is creative in his language use, he does not say *patience must you have* or even *patience you have must*. The reason for this is that the two words *must have* have to appear in this order in statements in English. They make up the 'verbal' element of the clause, forming a so-called verb phrase.

Exercise 6.1

Think about the following clause: *The little girl holds a green balloon*. Could this clause be expressed in any of the following alternatives? Why or why not?

a   *Balloon girl holds little the green a.*
b   *The girl little holds a balloon green.*
c   *A green balloon the little girl holds.*
d   *A green balloon holds the little girl.*

I am sure you will agree that example (a) is gibberish, a random order of words. We can guess that the balloon is green, rather than the girl, but it is unclear whether the adjective *little* refers to balloon or girl. Similarly, we may guess which nouns the definite and indefinite articles relate to, yet this is not clear from the way the words are arranged. We need to see articles, adjectives and nouns grouped together into *noun phrases*.

Example (b) is a bit easier to understand, as the noun phrases are grouped together correctly, forming a <u>subject noun phrase</u> *the girl little* and an <u>object noun phrase</u> *a balloon green*. Yet, within the noun phrases, the order of adjective and noun is odd. In English, adjectives precede nouns. Yet, in other languages, such as Portuguese, adjectives may follow nouns; e.g. *a menina pequena* (literally 'the girl little'). It is possible that a non-native speaker of English could utter this clause, using the structures they know from their own language, yet it is unlikely that an English speaker would do so.

In example (c), the individual words within the noun phrases *a green balloon* and *the little girl* are grouped together and the order within each noun phrase is right (e.g. the indefinite article *a* precedes the adjective *green*, which in turn precedes the noun *balloon*). The overall order of subject, verb and object is not standard SVO, but rather OSV, as in our Yoda example above. Hence, in certain situations, such as when contrasting the balloons with something else, this kind of clause would be fully acceptable by native speakers of English.

Finally, in example (d), a slightly different order of subject, verb and object is used, namely OVS. Could you think of any circumstances in which this clause is used? While some native speakers of English may even accept this order, most others would probably judge it dubious or plain wrong.

We saw in the exercise that subject, verb and object can consist of more than one word, and that these words generally appear in a certain order. In linguistics, we use the term *constituent* to refer to phrases that function at sentence level. Hence, a subject constituent is a noun phrase that functions as the subject of a clause (independent of the number of words it contains). Subsequently, linguists tend to prefer the term *constituent order* to word order, because strictly speaking it is the order of the constituents (subject, verb, object) we are looking at, rather than the order of individual words.

6.2 PHRASES

So far we have seen a number of examples of noun phrases in different functions. Noun phrases may contain just one word (such as *Maya* or *you* in the examples above) or more than one word (such as *the little girl*). In the previous section, we learnt that the words in a noun phrase have to appear in a certain order in English to be considered 'correct', while other orders may be understood but not considered native-like English, such as **the girl little*. In English, the main noun *girl* – also called the *head* noun – of the noun phrase appears after elements such as *the* and *little*.

When articles like *the* appear in a noun phrase they are usually referred to as determiners. The reason for using the term determiner for this slot in the noun phrase is that a number of elements belonging to other word classes can appear there as well. For example, we can replace *the* by a *numeral one*, a demonstrative pronoun *that* or a possessive pronoun *our*: *the little girl*, *one little girl*, *that little girl*, *our little girl*.

The other element, *little*, is an adjective. Within the noun phrase, it fulfils a specific function, namely telling us more about the head noun *girl*; in a way, specifying or *modifying* the noun, acting as a *modifier* to the noun. For this reason, it is also referred to as a modifier in the noun phrase.[2]

We can also identify other phrases: verb phrases, such as *must have* in the example above or adverb phrases, such as *very slowly*. This is an adverb phrase because the word that carries the main meaning (the head) is the adverb *slowly*. *Very* is a modifier in this case, telling us more about the head.

Exercise 6.2

Identify the types of phrases given below, underlining the head of each phrase:

a   *a big balloon*
b   *very carefully*
c   *the generous offer*
d   *has been seen*
e   *really slowly*
f   *very slow*

The head words in these examples happen to be the last elements in each example: *balloon* (noun), *carefully* (adverb), *offer* (noun), *seen* (verb), *slowly* (adverb) and *slow* (adjective). The phrases are thus noun phrase, adverb phrase, noun phrase, verb phrase, adverb phrase and adjective phrase.

6.3 SUBJECTS AND OBJECTS

In chapter 4, I introduced transitivity, which relates to how many noun phrases a verb needs to appear with to make sense. Intransitive verbs such as *run* only appear with a *subject* (*the girl* ran). Transitive verbs such as *kiss* appear with a subject and an object (*she* kissed *him*) and ditransitive verbs appear with a subject and two objects (*she* gave **HIM the present**). These two objects are sometimes referred to as direct object ('the present') and *indirect object* ('him'). Ditransitive verbs tend to be less frequent overall than transitive and intransitive verbs.

Subjects and objects are often distinguished in the languages of the world by the category of case, but how this is done can vary a lot. Let us briefly look at case marking in English:

(34a)	*The man*	*walks.*	
(34b)	*He*	*walks.*	
(35a)	*The man*	*sees*	*the woman.*
(35b)	*He*	*sees*	**her.**
(36a)	*The woman*	*sees*	*the man.*
(36b)	*She*	*sees*	**him.**

In English, case is only marked on certain personal pronouns (such as *I, she, we*), and not nouns. Hence part (a) of the examples above displays no case marking, as the subject and object noun phrases do not contain pronouns. In part (b) of each example, the subject and object noun phrases contain pronouns, and we are likely to find case marking. The subjects of intransitive verbs (34b) and transitive verbs (35b and 36b) are all relatively straightforward – they appear in the so-called *nominative* case. The objects in (35b) and (36b), on the other hand, are in the object case, the *accusative*. *Her* (35b) is different from *she* (36b). The object form *him* (36b) contrasts with the subject form *he* (35b).[3]

Some languages mark all subject and objects for case, while others have no or only very restricted case marking similar to English. In some languages, like German, case is indicated as agreement (see chapter 5) on determiners and modifiers in a noun phrase, such as (*ich sehe*) *den grossen Hund* '(I see) the big dog' where *den* 'the' and *grossen* 'big' mark for the accusative case in German, which indicates that *Hund* 'dog' is the object of the clause. German also uses an additional case, the *dative*, to mark indirect objects as well as elements appearing after certain prepositions such as *zu* 'to', as in *zu dem Haus* 'to the house'. Here the definite article *dem* marks for singular, masculine and dative case in agreement with the noun *Haus*. You can see from this example that case can also appear under other circumstances than just marking subjects and objects.

6.4 SEMANTIC ROLES

On the basis of our examples so far, we could assume the subjects are always people consciously carrying out the action described by the verb. But is that really so?

Exercise 6.3

Look at the following intransitive verbs and their subject. What type of subject is it, and how does the subject relate to the verbal meaning? (subjects in **bold**)

The old man walked.
He slept.
The cat purred.
The book fell off the table.

Now look at the following transitive verbs and their subject and objects. How can we classify the subject and object in relation to the verbal meaning? (subjects in **bold**, objects underlined)

He bought cake.
They received the letter.
The ball hit a wall.
The breeze caught her hair.

In *the old man walked* and *he bought cake*, the subjects are indeed consciously carrying out an action. But it is less clear what the involvement of the subject is in *he slept*, let alone *they received a letter*. In the latter, the subject certainly did not have to act as such, but was the recipient of some sort. It gets even more complicated when the subject is a thing, such as *the ball* or *the breeze*, which are not able to act consciously.

The way to get around this is to look at subjects and objects in terms of their meaning in the clause, referred to as *semantic roles*. Traditionally, these include *agents* (those acting, like *the old man*), *patients* (those being affected by an action, e.g. being bought, like *the cake*), *recipients* (as *they*, our letter recipients in the example) and more. We can then, also, take into account the meaning of the verbs in relation to their subject (and object). Is it an action, such as *buying*, or an event such as the book *falling* off the table?

6.5 PREDICATES

We saw above that clauses have subjects and we learnt that these are often – but far from always – noun phrases referring to someone doing something. The rest of the clause is less standardized: some clauses contain objects, others just a verb, a reference to a place, sometimes we find copular verbs followed by adjectives (see section 4.6) or other constructions. Overall, this part of the clause is characterized by the verb and whichever other elements appear with it. In traditional grammar, it is referred to as the *predicate*. The predicate accompanies the subject and tells us what the subject is up to. The types of predicates we can find in language are quite diverse.

Thus, in clauses the predicate consists of a verb and, maybe, an object (37). In copular clauses the predicate can contain an adjective (38) or a noun (39). In both types of clauses the predicate can hold other information, such as adverbs (40), or additional information expressed in English through phrases introduced by prepositions (41–42).

(37) She **bought ice-cream.**
(38) She **is young.**
(39) She **is a teacher.**
(40) She **is here.**
(41) She **is in the room.**
(42) She **sings in the chapel.**

In each of these examples, the predicates are presented in bold. Put in simple terms, the predicate is everything that is not the subject – it relates to the rest of the clause that, under normal circumstances, contains the verb.[4]

6.6 OTHER SYNTACTIC CONCEPTS: QUESTIONS, NEGATION, VOICE

There are a number of other common concepts that affect sentences. These include questions, negation and *voice*. Questions, or *interrogative clauses* can be formed in different ways across the languages of the world. Often, languages use interrogative pronouns, such as the English wh-elements *who, which, how, where* (see chapter 4). Such questions are also called content-questions, as they ask about a specific piece of information. The answer may consist of just that one piece of information, such as:

(43a) *Where are you?* **Here.**
(44a) *Where did you go?* **The zoo.**

This answer suffices, and is often given rather than a whole clause such as *You are here* or *We went to the zoo.* There are also yes–no questions, which can be answered simply by 'yes' or 'no', or by 'yes' or 'no' with further explanations:

(45a) *Are you tired?* **No.**
(46a) *Do you want to eat something?* **Yes, I'm actually quite hungry.**

In English, as well as some other languages, questions are formed with inversion. This concept needs some further explanation. Let us start with the corresponding *declarative* clauses to the questions given above, compared to those questions:

(43b)	*You are here.*	*Where are you?*
(44b)	*You went to the zoo.*	*Where did you go?*
(45b)	*You are tired.*	*Are you tired?*
(46b)	*You want to eat something.*	*Do you want to eat something?*

In the wh-questions (43) and (44) the wh-element appears at the beginning of the clause. In (43) the subject *you* and the verb *are* are in a different order in the question. While the declarative clause on the left has *you are*, the question on the right is *are you*. This switch, if you like, is called inversion. The same is the case in (45), where *you are* of the declarative clause turns into *are you* in the interrogative clause. Examples (44) and (46) have an additional element of complication, which is quite specific to English. In this case, the generic verb *do* is used to carry out the inversion – which is also referred to as *do-support* in English.[5] There are also other ways in which questions are formed in the languages of the world, and even in English. Content questions may be asked by replacing the element asked about with a question word in its regular place in the clause, such as *You asked **what** of her?* in informal English.[6]

In some ways, questions are similar to negation, at least in English. Negation is another category where do-support and inversion takes place:

(47a) *He bought a car.*
(47b) *He **did not** buy a car.*

Again, when the clause contains a copular verb or an auxiliary verb, the negative element can be added without any addition of *do*:

(48a) *He had **not** understood the task.*
(48b) *He had understood the task.*
(49a) *He is **not** tall.*
(49b) *He is tall.*

English is special, in this case, and in some languages of the world a negative element is simply placed in front of the element being negated, without any do-inversion or the like. Yet, there are many other ways in which negation can be marked and languages differ greatly.

Finally, voice is another way in which elements of a sentence can be moved around, taken in and out of focus. In English, we have the *passive voice*. It is quite a useful syntactic structure if you want to focus or blame away from something:

(50a) *I ate the cake.*
(50b) *The cake was eaten (by someone).*

In this case, the 'original' *active* clause subject *I* and object *the cake* have been moved around. We can call *I* the *agent*, i.e. the element carrying out the action, and *the cake* the *patient*, i.e. the element undergoing some change. This patient, *the cake*, has now become the subject of the clause, while the agent *I* is absent. It may be mentioned as an add-on, in a so-called *by-phrase*, but this is not necessary. Rather, the focus is now on what happened to the patient, *the cake*, in this case. The active transitive clause with subject and object has, at the same time, become an intransitive clause with only a subject. The passive is quite a common voice structure in the languages of the world, but there are also other categories such as causatives (expressing who caused an action to happen) and similar.

6.7 COMPLEX SENTENCES: COORDINATION AND SUBORDINATION

So far we have dealt with simple sentences, those that have a subject and a predicate. Now, it is time to move on to combinations of clauses. Complex sentences are those that include more than one predicate. There are two ways in which clauses can be combined: *coordination* and *subordination*.

Coordination refers to the combination of two (or more) clauses (or, indeed other elements such as phrases) at the same level. A coordination of clauses is the following:

(51) *She wanted an ice-cream but he ordered a lemonade.*

Here two clauses (1) *She wanted an ice-cream* and (2) *He ordered a lemonade* are put together. Grammatically, there is no dependence of one clause on another other than *but* in the middle, which indicates that the two clauses are connected. There are three such *coordinating conjunctions* in English *and, or, but.*

The other way in which clauses can be put together is by subordination. In this case, one clause is dependent on another. An example is:

(52) *She said **that she wanted an ice-cream**.*

In this case, we have an overall clause *she said (something)*, and another clause that goes into detail with what she said: *that she wanted an ice-cream*. The latter clause (given in bold print) is subordinated to the first one, and there is a grammatical dependency between these two clauses.

This is one type of subordination, which we call a *complement clause*. In this case, the subordinate clause is the object of the *main clause she said (something = that she wanted an ice-cream).* There are two other types of subordinate clauses in English. *Adverbial* clauses give extra information, such as about the time, manner, place, purpose, reason or condition of the action:

(53) *He ordered lemonade **because he was thirsty**.*

The subordinate clause, which is presented in bold here, gives us more information about what happened in the main clause – in this case the reasoning for his order.

The other type of subordinate clause is a *relative clause*. Remember our discussion of noun phrases – and adjectives as modifiers in noun phrases. Such modifiers in noun phrases can also be whole clauses, so-called *relative clauses*. An example is:

(54) *The pupil **who brought his graffiti gear to school** may face expulsion.*

Again, the subordinate clause (a relative clause) is presented in bold. In this case, it contains a subject and a predicate – which means it is a clause. At the same time, however, it functions as a modifier in the noun phrase, telling us more about which *pupil* we are talking about. Thereby, its function is very similar to that of an adjective in a noun phrase. Compare, for example, *the naughty pupil*, where *naughty* has a similar modifying function to the relative clause in the example above.

Exercise 6.4

For the following examples, decide whether the clauses are coordinated or subordinated. If you feel courageous, you can additionally try to decide the types of subordination given:

a *She thought that the butterflies would not fly at this time of the day.*
b *When I walk along this path I feel happy.*
c *Should we go to the seaside today or would you prefer a hike in the hills?*
d *It was a lovely party, because all my friends were there.*
e *My new rucksack, which comes with a bottle holder, is not much better than the old one that I was replacing.*
f *There is not much to see when it is raining and the windows are steamed up.*

Coordinated clauses can be easy to find when *and, or* or *but* are present, as in examples (c) and (f) above. The remaining clauses are subordinations. In (a) *that* introduces a complement clause. In (b) *when* tells us something about the time, introducing an adverbial clause. In a similar way *because* in (d) gives us a reason and introduces another adverbial clause. There are two relative clauses in (e), introduced by *which* and *that*. Both give more information about the rucksacks talked about.

Additionally, did you spot the subordination in (f) that appears alongside the coordinated clauses? *When* is introducing the adverbial subordinate clause(s), and *and* coordinates the two adverbial clauses *it is raining* and *the windows are steamed up*?

FURTHER READING

The study of sentence structures, syntax, is one of the areas of linguistics with the widest gap between individual approaches. You can pick up two introductory books to the field only to find out that they have very little or even nothing at all in common. Each approach to syntax has its own terminology and this is sometimes highly complex and formalized.

An excellent general introduction to the field that provides the basic without favouring one particular theory is Tallerman (2014) *Understanding syntsax*. Most introductory books on linguistics include information about syntax, such as Yule (2014) *The study of language*. Just like introductions to morphological structures in the world's languages, introductions to linguistic typology provide information about sentence structures, for example Velupillai (2012) *An introduction to linguistic typology* and Moravcsik (2012) *Introducing language typology*.

NOTES

1   This verb is *inflected*, appearing with the -*s* that marks a third person singular subject in the present tense. Verbs that are inflected are also referred to as *finite verbs*, as opposed to *non-finite verbs* such as infinitives.

2   Determiners and modifiers are not heads of a phrase. Such elements are often referred to as the *dependents*.

3   Notice that *you*, again, is different. It is not only the same for singular and plural, but also for nominative and accusative case: I see *you* (object), *You* see me (subject).

4   There are so-called nominal clauses that do not contain verbs. Also, some languages such as Russian do not use the copular verb *be* in the present tense, but rather put subject and *predicative adjective* (or noun) together without any verbal element present. 'She is young' would thus be *ona* **molodaja** (literally 'she young') in Russian. In this case, the predicate consists of *molodaja* 'young' without a separate verb.

5   This type of do-support happens with all verbs that are not copular verbs and that do not appear with auxiliaries. When auxiliary verbs are present, the auxiliaries take part in the inversion, such as *He has eaten.* → **Has** *he eaten?* Note that the auxiliary verb *has* is inverted, while the main verb *eaten* remains in its regular place. In British English it is also possible to say this with a non-auxiliary *have*, such as *have you anything to say?* in which case *have* is the main verb.

6   In this case, the wh-element is usually stressed.

Meaning and discourse

IN THIS CHAPTER

Meaning is integral to language. Without meaning language is little more than noise. While all modern approaches to language, irrespective of the theoretical perspective, take into account meaning, this has not always been the case. Some older theories of grammar (we will come back to some of this in chapter 8) have treated constructions such as the famous *Colourless green ideas sleep furiously* as syntactically well-formed, despite not making sense to speakers of the language.

In this chapter, I will explore a number of aspects relating to meaning, from individual words through larger constructs to connectivity in discourse:

- Lexical meaning: literal and non-literal, metaphor, metonymy

- Polysemy and homonymy

- Sense relations: synonymy, antonymy and hyponymy

- Sentence level meaning: inference, proposition and presupposition

- Meaning and context: pragmatics

- Discourse.

7.1 LEXICAL MEANING

In my opinion, having a good dictionary when learning a new language can be a big advantage. Whenever I come across a word I do not know, I can simply look it up in the dictionary and, most likely, find out what it means. So far so good, but what if a word has many different translations? Imagine a speaker of another language who has just started learning English and does not understand the word *over*. He looks it up in a dictionary, which gives a range of meanings, including 'above' (as in *You can place this hook **over the door***) and 'above and across' (*She jumped **over the fence***). He remembers this as *over* meaning 'above, with or without movement across', or short 'above +/− movement'. Our learner will probably have no difficulty with these two different, albeit related meanings of the word. However, what will he do when he encounters *over* in other environments?

Exercise 7.1

Have a look at the following uses of *over* in different contexts. How would you describe the meaning of the word in these environments? Would you be able to relate it to the meaning identified as 'above, +/– movement'?

a   *She walked all **over** him.*
b   ***over** the moon*
c   ***over** there*
d   *It is all **over.***
e   (in radio communication) ***over!***

If you look up *over* in a dictionary, you are likely to find many different entries for the word. Indeed, one of the freely available online dictionaries lists 50 different constructions in which *over* appears. Some of these uses are quite far removed from what we could abbreviate as 'above, +/- movement' sense of *over*. While *she walked all over him* could be construed as 'above + movement across' similar to *jump over the fence*, the meaning is non-literal in this case, or so we would hope. Words can have *literal* meanings (in the case of *she walked all over him* he would be lying down and she would be standing on top of him, walking back and forth) or non-literal meanings, also called *metaphorical* or figurative meanings (in this case she would have been overbearing towards him, as if she had walked across him, while no 'walking' as such was involved). Another example of a *metaphor* is (b) *over the moon*. Again, we may be able to think about a literal sense in which this expression is used, such as a rocket in flight, seen from Earth. Still, but the metaphorical sense is likely to be the most frequent way this expression is used.

Just like metaphor, *metonymy* also refers to something – in this case a name – without mentioning it directly, using non-literal language. For example, **Buckingham Palace** *was not amused* does not literally mean that the real estate itself thought this way, but rather refers to its inhabitants. Metonymy thus affects the naming of people or institutions. Likewise, when we talk about *Hollywood* we tend to refer to a specific aspect of the American film industry, rather than merely a place in California.

Example (c) *over there* is a far stretch from 'above +/- movement', as it refers to a place at a certain distance. We may, perhaps, be able to relate it to the 'across' aspect of *over*, but even that is not closely linked to the core meaning of the word identified above. Finally, (d) and (e) are even further removed. *It is all over* and *over!* in radio communication relate to 'done, finished'. In this case, we may argue, we are not dealing with the original word *over* at all, but rather with a separate word written and pronounced the same way, but with an entirely different meaning.

We can say that *over* presents a case of *polysemy* in that it has various, but related meanings: (1) stationary 'above' *over the door*, (2) 'movement above and across' *over the fence* and perhaps even (3) 'across' *over there*. Another example of polysemy is the word *wood*, which can refer to an area with many trees, as well as to a much smaller element, e.g. a piece of a tree: *a piece of wood*. Such polysemy often arises because language changes over time and words can take on different, yet related meanings.

Still, new meanings can also arise. In this way, you can check the history of the language in the *OED* and find that *over* in the sense of 'finished' is first testified from 1611, with two dubious uses in the two centuries prior to that. We may want to treat *over* in the sense of 'finished' as a separate word, because of its difference in meaning. Linguists refer to this as a *homonym*. Homonyms have the same form in writing (referred to as *homographs*) and pronunciation (referred to as *homophones*). Even though they may be historically linked, their modern meanings are unrelated. Another example of a homonym is *down*, which can be a preposition or adverb referring to a direction, or a type of (fluffy) feather.

7.2 SYNONYMY, ANTONYMY, HYPONYMY

So far we have mainly looked at the polysemous, homonymous and metaphorical senses of a single word, *over*. There are also ways in which meanings of different words can relate to one another. For example, words that mean more or less the same thing are usually referred to as *synonyms*. Examples include *sofa, couch* and *settee*. You may prefer to use just one of these, which may have something to do with your age or the variety of English you speak. Yet, all three expressions refer to a specific item of furniture and are used by speakers of contemporary English.

Another way to refer to a relationship in meaning between two words is *antonymy*, which refers to opposite meanings such as *good* and *bad*. The term *hypernym* refers to a generic word that can have various *hyponyms*, words that refer to more specific entities within that overall meaning. For example, *wood anemone* is a type of *anemone*, which in turn is a type of *flower*. Hence, *wood anemone* is a hyponym of *anemone*, which in turn is a hyponym of *flower*. Or, the other way around, the term *flower* is a hypernym for words referring to specific flowers.

7.3 THE LOGIC OF LANGUAGE: INFERENCE, PROPOSITION AND PRESUPPOSITION

Philosophers – both ancient and modern – are often drawn to language, looking at what constitutes meaning, and how language, in an abstract sense, is linked to the world around us. A great part of this constitutes the study of *logic*. We may argue that logic is inherent to language, and concepts like *inference* play an important role. A typical inference is of the type *All X are Y. Z is an X, hence Z is Y.* For example:

(55a)   *All children like sweets.*
(55b)   *Becky is a child.*
(55c)   *Hence: Becky likes sweets.*

The inference lies in having just stated that all of a group do something, hence we would expect parts of the group would do the same.

The three different statements in the example can be referred to as *propositions*. This is a term that is used in a number of ways in linguistics, usually referring to a 'statement' or a 'clause'.[1] The inference arises from the combination of these three propositions. They appear together, hence we expect the things they express to relate to one another.

Just like with inference, there are other concepts of logic that play a role in the way language is understood. The concept of *presupposition*, for example, describes an underlying assumption that may not be mentioned directly:

(56) *It wasn't me who left the door open.*

This sentence presupposes that the door was left open, thus by uttering this statement we assume that the door was left open. We cannot, however, be sure who is to blame – someone may have accidentally or deliberately left it open, the wind may have pushed the door open or even 'I' in the statement above may ultimately be responsible.

Assumptions expressed through presuppositions can be very subtle, and hence this can be a strong tool in steering people towards a certain opinion, for example in political propaganda.

There can be a big difference between the *logical* approach to language and the way language works in reality. For example, the use of a double negative (57b) could be interpreted with a positive reading:

(57a) *He has **nothing** to fear.*
(57b) *He hasn't got **nothing** to fear.*

People may argue that (57b) is not logical because the two negations cancel each other out, turning this into a (false) positive. Yet, the way languages work can be different from mathematical logic. For example, in (57b) the two parts of the negation *-n't* and *nothing* appear together as one negative entity, rather than two separate negations. For the speaker who utters (57b) this is a strengthening of the negation, rather than a false, 'logical' positive. Notice also that some languages, such as French, use double negations as part of their standard grammar. In example (58) the negative elements are highlighted in bold:

(58) *Il*   *n'a*   ***rien***   *à*   *craindre.*
         He   NEG-have.3SG   nothing   to   fear.INF
         'He has nothing to fear.'

7.4 MEANING AND CONTEXT: PRAGMATICS

So far we have looked at a number of areas of semantics, dealing with the underlying meaning of words and propositions. Meaning can, however, also be broader and extend beyond the sentence, arising from the overall discourse context. This is what the study of pragmatics is about.

To look at a simple case where meaning interacts with the overall discourse context, let me start with the concept of *deixis*. Quite a few expressions in a language are anchored in the immediate discourse context, and are thereby deictic. For example, personal pronouns like *I* and *you* are dependent on who utters them. They can refer to different people, depending on who is talking. *I*, in this way, refers to the person speaking, the second person *you* is a person addressed by the speaker, while the third person pronouns *he*, *she* and *it* refer to referents outside of the discourse context. When somebody else starts speaking, *I* automatically refers to them. If you want, *I* is at the centre of our focus, and is therefore also referred to as the *deictic centre* in person deixis. There are other types of deixis as well, such as temporal and spatial deixis.

Exercise 7.2

Think about the concept of *deictic centre*. What do you think is the deictic centre referring to 'time'? What is the deictic centre for 'place'?

Temporal deixis refers to time. When we say *yesterday*, we usually see this word in relation to *now*, or rather the time of speaking. Speaking about *tomorrow* depends, again, on the time of the utterance. Napoleon or some other historical figure talking about *tomorrow* will refer to a time in the future dependent on their own *now*, that is the deictic centre, while this may be a long way in the past for us. Spatial deixis, likewise, refers to the place in relation to the discourse context. *Here* and *there* are linked to their context, with *here* referring to the deictic centre and *there* to a place that is not the deictic centre.

Sometimes the use of deictic elements can lead to ambiguity. For example, a note on a door saying *I will be back in 5 minutes* needs to be read within its context. Imagine it is the door of a single-occupancy office, in which case *I* will, most likely, refer to the occupant of the office. *Back*, likewise, will refer to the office, or rather '*here*' at the deictic centre where the note is placed. *5 minutes* may pose more of a problem for the person reading the note, as we do not know when this note was written. It can get even more difficult when you get a text message from a number you do not recognize stating *I am here, where are you?* In this case, again, the discourse context may still provide an answer to the question, but if that is not the case, you may be left puzzled.

7.5 TEXTS: COHERENCE AND COHESION

Large chunks of language beyond the limits of the sentence are also referred to as *texts*. Texts can be written, signed or spoken. There are two ways in which texts are linked together and make sense in terms of their meaning. The two concepts behind this are *coherence* and *cohesion*.

Coherence refers to the logic of a sentence linked to the underlying meaning and context conveyed. This means, the text is logically built up and the different parts of the text relate to one another. In common language, we use the term *coherent* to refer to just that.

Cohesion, on the other hand, is a less commonly used term, yet it holds some importance in linguistics. A cohesive text links different elements across sentences in such a way that the text makes sense. For example, introducing a new referent such as *the man*, we can refer to this referent with a personal pronoun *he* in the following context. *He* is in this case referring to an entity introduced in the previous context; linguists call this phenomenon *anaphora*. Anaphora ensures links across the text. Inference plays a role as well. Since *the man* was introduced in a previous proposition, we infer that when a pronoun *he* is used in the same context, it is in reference to *the man* (or another third person already introduced in the context).

7.6 THE ANALYSIS OF DISCOURSE

A popular topic in modern linguistics is the analysis of discourse. Approaches to discourse analysis typically examine the ways in which speakers interact in different situations, using natural language, which requires careful recording of what is said. A concept of discourse analysis is, for example, *turn-taking*. Imagine a dialogue in a movie or a theatre play. Typically, actors have their *turn*, which means they speak. Then, in an orderly manner, the next actor has their say. Natural language does not always work that way. Next time you are witnessing a heated debate, try to listen out for overlap in people's speech.

Exercise 7.3

Watch a television debate or panel show, such as *Question Time* or something similar, and note down which mechanisms panellists employ to 'keep their turn', that is to keep speaking. Then, focus on the techniques used by others trying to 'get a turn', that is trying to speak.

The type of discourse behaviour you get depends a lot on the situation. Yet, in your analysis of discourse behaviour in a debate, you probably noticed that when speakers try to maintain their turn, they speak faster and try to avoid breaks at the ends of sentences so that others do not take over their turn. Those that are keen to take a turn will, likewise, employ a range of strategies to get noticed. That could be clearing their throat as if preparing to speak, using discourse markers such as *well, sure, but*, or eventually interrupting the person speaking in order to be able to speak.

FURTHER READING

There are many introductory books to the studies of semantics, pragmatics and discourse. These include Birner (2012) *Introduction to pragmatics*, Cutting (2007) *Pragmatics and discourse*, Jones (2012) *Discourse analysis: a resource book for students*, Löbner (2013) *Understanding semantics*, Paltridge (2012) *Discourse analysis* and Senft (2014) *Understanding pragmatics*. Cruse's (2011) *Meaning in language* combines the studies of semantics and pragmatics and deals with the central concepts in these fields.

NOTE

1   Sometimes, linguists look at such *propositional logic*, i.e. the relationships between statements or clauses. Yet, there is also *predicate logic*, which looks at the logical relationships within a clause.

Understanding approaches to language

Theory and practice

IN THIS CHAPTER

This chapter is about different approaches to linguistic data. By the end of the chapter, you will have an understanding of a number of ways in which researchers develop new knowledge and you will be able to evaluate such research, for example when confronted with a range of opinions on the same linguistic phenomena. My aim is to get you to think critically about what you read and to form your own opinions about presentations of specific ideas you come across. This chapter contains in particular:

- How to critically evaluate reports about language in the media and elsewhere

- The Chomsky–Everett debate about linguistic complexity

- Theoretical linguistics

- Descriptive linguistics

- Differences between approaches to language

8.1 REPORTS ON RESEARCH

The media is full of stories about new discoveries: caves that have revealed ancient human remains, DNA sequences that allow us to understand previously untreatable diseases, new planets discovered in the outer reaches of our galaxy. And, from time to time, such discoveries relate to language. They include, for example, reports on studies into the sounds cows produce, copying the intonation of their farmers, or reports about presidents' discourse strategies revealing information about hidden agendas. Sometimes, even grammars of languages make the news. One such example is Pirahã, a language spoken by a few hundred indigenous people in the Brazilian Amazon.

The Pirahã language was discussed in a range of media reports following the publication of two research articles outlining surprising linguistic features. One such feature is the lack of numerals, i.e. words for one, two, three, and the related fact that the Pirahã do not count. Another unexpected feature is the comparatively simple structure of phrases and sentences in the language, without any *recursion*, such as the subordination of clauses (see chapter 6). This claim, first brought forward by Dan Everett in 2005, caused a major debate in the field of linguistics. The main reason for this was that the claim contradicted the latest version of a prominent theory about language developed by the linguist Noam Chomsky. Together with two colleagues, Chomsky had put forward a claim in 2002 that all human languages exhibit recursion, which is what sets human languages apart from animal communication (in Hauser, Chomsky & Fitch 2002).[1]

Exercise 8.1

Before you read on, think about the following:

1   How can we find out who is right? Everett or Chomsky?

2   Chomsky hypothesized that all human languages exhibit recursion. How did he arrive at this idea, and how can he test it (do you think he looked at all of the 6,000+ spoken languages of the world)?

3   Working on the Pirahã language for a few decades during which he had learnt to speak the language fluently, Everett proposed that it exhibits no recursive structures. Can we believe what he says?

I will come back to the questions of the last exercise in the text below.

8.2 THEORIES, HYPOTHESES AND GAINING NEW INSIGHTS

I used the terms *theory* and *hypothesis* above, without much explanation. Sometimes, especially in everyday speech, these terms are used interchangeably. Yet, in academic language use, we tend to distinguish between the two. In a nutshell, a hypothesis is usually smaller and less tested than a theory. So, if you write an essay (cf. chapter 9), you may start with an outline of your hypothesis, which you would then test, or at least discuss, in the remainder of the essay. Thus, a hypothesis is an idea that needs to be tested and confirmed. Once established, it may become a 'theory'.[2] A theory is hence a recognized and verified hypothesis. It usually takes considerably longer for such a theory to develop.

Coming back to our linguistic controversy, Chomsky had built up a theory of language,[3] starting with work he conducted in the 1950s. The theory was based on a range of hypotheses about languages. Initially most of the languages used to test these hypotheses were very similar in structure, and related to English. In later decades this was extended to a much wider range of languages of the world. The 'theory' subsequently underwent a number of innovations and changes to take into account the new findings that we arrived at by analysing the language data. For example, initially Chomsky and colleagues presented a much longer list of features typical of human languages. These had more or less been reduced to 'recursion' as the only such feature in the beginning of the millennium.

One reason why Everett's claim about the lack of recursion in Pirahã was contentious to followers of Chomsky was the fact that by disproving the last remaining feature on which the theory was built, the entire theory was disproved. That is, in the terminology above, if the Pirahã facts are right, Chomsky's approach would be a mere hypothesis that has been shown to be wrong by data from one small Amazonian language. This issue highlights that using absolute statements such as "a certain feature will exist in human languages" can be dangerous, as this claim can, in principle, be disproved by a single language.

The controversy will continue until we reach new hypotheses and theoretical insights. Other researchers have tested the Pirahã data, and they will continue to add their arguments to the debate. Also, other languages have been brought into the debate. Through continuous testing of hypotheses and verification of findings we can drive forward a theory, and get further insights into how language functions, and ultimately whether or not language is a feature that distinguishes humans from other living beings.

8.3 EMPIRICAL AND THEORETICAL APPROACHES

Let us now look at this in terms of the ways in which Chomsky and Everett work, which are quite different.

Chomsky used the so-called *top-down*, 'theoretical', approach. He developed hypotheses about what language is like, and then tested these on languages, forming his theory. Thus, the hypothesis was there first. Then, it was tested on actual language data. A theoretical linguist thus thinks about possible connections and comes up with hypotheses. Subsequently, she or he tests these hypotheses.

Everett, on the other hand, used the *bottom-up*, 'empirical', approach in his research on Pirahã. He worked on the language in detail, and described and analysed the features he found. Then, he compared what he had found to other languages and to hypotheses and theories presented in the literature. Thus, Everett did not have a hypothesis to begin with, but rather let the data guide him in his analysis. An empirical linguist looks at data in detail and formulates a hypothesis or even theory based on the data he or she has analysed.

The top-down and bottom-up approaches are two different ways in which to conduct research. Researchers are sometimes in favour of one of these approaches. Ultimately, both views are important in driving innovation. Top-down approaches open our perspectives for what we could look out for in languages. Bottom-up approaches bring up unexpected results, which drive forward ideas for theory development.

Thus, in order to analyse language systematically, we need both top-down and bottom-up approaches. Often, theory development takes time, and could be compared to a maze with many dead ends and corners that lead to unexpected places.

8.4 THEORETICAL LINGUISTICS

The field of theoretical linguistics consists of many different theoretical approaches and ideas about language. The picture becomes even more complicated when we look at the historical perspective, in that approaches to language have changed over time. According to the philosopher Kuhn (1962), researchers work in so-called paradigms, which are the common, underlying assumptions and research traditions at any one time across a field or even a number of fields. While many linguists worked in the paradigm called *Behaviourism* until the mid-twentieth century, Chomsky's and other generativists' work on language led to a paradigm shift in the field. A large number of linguists started to work on the assumption that language is innate, facilitated by a *language acquisition device* of some sort that is already present in the brain at the time of birth. Since then, a number of approaches to language have challenged the concept of innateness, as we saw above. Approaches to language change and can differ quite profoundly.

When referring to theoretical linguistics as such, we can be talking about quite different things. We can mean 'as different to mere description', or we can refer to a specific syntactic theory, such as *Minimalism*, Lexical Functional Grammar, Role and Reference Grammar just to name a few (see chapter 2).

8.5 DESCRIPTIVE LINGUISTICS

Some areas of linguistics can be very practical, while others are much more rooted in theory. For example, in practice-oriented approaches to language, such as the field of applied linguistics or language documentation and description, you may be more likely to come across practical, descriptive work that does not necessarily follow or test one particular theory.

For example, my own work on the grammar of Mosetén was a highly descriptive task. I went to the Amazonian area of Bolivia to conduct fieldwork on this indigenous language, which was previously mostly spoken rather than written and had not been analysed in detail. Collecting data and analysing these in order to describe most accurately the structures of the language, I aimed to present the data so that they would be relevant to all linguists, independent of their theoretical background. Much of the grammar relies on my own interpretations of the language data, but I was very careful to avoid a theoretical bias.

Having said that, sometimes the terminology available to us can greatly restrict us in how we describe the world around us.[4] In the case of grammar, much of the terminology we use arises from classical studies of Classical Greek, Latin and even Sanskrit, an ancient language from the Indian subcontinent related to modern Hindi. Terms such as case, preposition and inflection all relate to concepts found in these languages. Since most Western languages are in the same Indo-European language family as these three classical languages, the terminology still works relatively well for languages such as English.[5] This terminology works less well for languages that are not related to Indo-European, which can have very different grammatical concepts.

Let us look at an example. Having learnt the term *genitive* for the *-'s* that is sometimes added to names to indicate possession (such as *John's*), we may think that we are dealing with another genitive marker when coming across an element that is also added to names indicating possession in another language. Yet, this marker may have a very different use in that language: in the Indo-European languages, the genitive marker is quite restricted in marking possession. In other languages, such as Mosetén, markers that look like a genitive take on very different functions. For example the Mosetén marker *–si´* can be used just like *-'s* in English: *John-si´ aka´* 'John's house'. Yet, *-si'* can be used in a whole range of other places, where it does not indicate possession at all, for example in *jaem´ -si´ pheyakdye´* 'a good story', the *-si´* element marks the adjective 'good', indicating that it refers to 'story'. Thus, we have to be careful when using terminology from one set of languages to describe other languages, as they can skew the way in which we are looking at those other languages. On the other hand, starting an investigation of a new language without the concepts worked out by linguists for other languages would be quite difficult, so the researcher has to negotiate a way in which existing concepts can be used as guidance without compromising the way the new language under investigation works.

8.6 LANGUAGE CHANGE AND PRESCRIPTIVE GRAMMAR

In chapter 2, I briefly introduced the concepts of descriptive and prescriptive grammar. Descriptive grammar, as discussed above, looks at the way language is used by the speakers. Prescriptive grammar, on the other hand, relates to a set of rules that set out how a language 'ought to be', such as grammar books for learning a foreign language or books about correct speech. These two perspectives are not mutually exclusive: some prescriptive approaches to language are based on an initial description of a language. However, since language is an organic entity that is constantly changing, this description can become a statement of language used at an earlier time. In the meantime, new words will have appeared in the language, as well as novel grammatical constructions. Some words will have changed their meanings gradually, and some grammatical structures may now be used differently from the initial description.

Sometimes, the grammatical 'rules' of a language are not based on the way speakers use – or used to use – a language at all. For example, the grammatical description of English is heavily influenced by Latin and Greek terminology. We used terms such as preposition, which is the Latin original. The term 'grammar' is based on the Classical Greek *grammatike*, which found its way into English through Latin and Old French. Since scholars used Latin and Greek terminology, the description of the English grammar was, in a way, formed by the available terminology. This led to extremes, such as rules 'not to split an infinitive'. *Split infinitive* refers to the situation where the infinitive marker *to* and the verb, e.g. *laugh* do not appear right next to one another. Thus, a statement such as *to randomly laugh* would break the rule of not splitting the infinitive, because the infinitive marker *to* and the verb *laugh* are 'split' by the adverb *randomly*. A prescriptivist may remind you to use the expression *to laugh randomly* instead. However, when we look at the development of the English language we can see that split infinitives have been around for a long time. Latin, however, does not have split infinitives. There is a simple reason for this: infinitives are marked by suffixes in Latin, not a separate word *to* as in English. Thus, *to laugh* in Latin is *ridere*, which consists of the stem *ride-* and the infinitive ending *-re*. This construction cannot be split, as it forms just one word. Yet, this rule that has nothing to do with the way the English language functions made its way into the prescriptive grammar of the language, and is now seen as 'correct' speech by many.

8.7 CRITICAL THINKING AND EVALUATION OF RESEARCH

Before concluding this chapter, allow me to return to the beginning of the chapter: to what degree can we trust what we read in the media or even what researchers publish? The picture is complex, as there are many different issues to keep in mind: researchers may be working within a specific theoretical framework or paradigm, which may skew their perspective on the data investigated. There may be a debate about the issue in question, and researchers can have widely different opinions about the interpretation of language data. Additionally, the data may be looked at in a selective manner, in that only those data that clearly prove (or disprove) a theory are highlighted. Or the data could have been collected in such a way that it would prove a theory. We will look in more detail at research methods in chapter 9, which will highlight a number of additional issues in the way language can be analysed and how results from such analyses can be interpreted.

Exercise 8.2

One of the claims about language that made it to the news was Keith Chen's argument that language and economics are linked. More precisely, the argument was that the likelihood of you saving money for the future depends on how your language expresses the future tense.

For this exercise, search online to find Chen's TED talk on the subject as well as reflections in blog posts and elsewhere published by linguists (such as on the linguistics blog *LanguageLog*). Then, make a list of the arguments in favour of Chen's claim and those against. Once you have done that, try to write a short paragraph to state your opinion on the matter (you could also talk to a friend and explain the situation and your take on the matter, if you prefer that).[6]

FURTHER READING

For an introduction to the debate between Everett and Chomsky on Pirahã, see Everett's (2009) personal account in *Don't sleep, there are snakes*. There are numerous easily accessible blog posts and online resources on the debate.

Most books on research methods go into further detail with hypotheses, such as Dörnyei (2007) *Research methods in applied linguistics*. See chapter 9 for further recommendations. Books about the history of linguistics will guide you through a range of theories and approaches to the field, for example Allan (2010) *The western classical tradition in linguistics*.

Language change is dealt with in many books from a range of areas of linguistics. For example, Baugh and Cable (2012) discuss the development and change experienced by the English language. Historical language change is dealt with in books on historical linguistics, for example Ringe and Eska (2013) *Historical linguistics*. If you are interested in variations in the language spoken today, books in sociolinguistics will provide more information, such as Aitchison (2012) *Language change: progress or decay?* and Meyerhoff (2011) *Introducing sociolinguistics*.

NOTES

1   The controversy is more complex than this and you are referred to the section on 'further reading' for more detailed information on the topic from a range of different perspectives.
2   The *Oxford English Dictionary* defines 'hypothesis' as: "A proposition or principle put forth or stated (without any reference to its correspondence with fact) merely as a basis for reasoning or argument, or as a premise from which to draw a conclusion; a supposition." A theory is defined as "a hypothesis that has been confirmed or established by observation or experiment, and is propounded or accepted as accounting for the known facts".
3   This approach was usually referred to as a 'theory', even though Chomsky used different terminology. He called the latest of his approaches the 'Minimalist Program' rather than the 'Minimalist Theory'.
4   This is another interesting subject, which linguists also study within the area of linguistics relativity.
5   Nonetheless, there are differences as well. Some concepts typical of ancient Indo-European languages, such as the subjunctive, are in decline in many modern Indo-European languages.
6   There is no clear answer to this question and it is up to you how you approach this topic. It may be enough to say that many linguists reject this claim, yet there may be a grain of truth in this matter after all. The debate on this and other claims continues.

Research methods

Collecting, analysing and presenting data

IN THIS CHAPTER

Is it possible for an undergraduate student to conduct research? The answer is a clear "yes, absolutely"! Learning to conduct a simple research project is part of most undergraduate degrees, and definitely something encouraged when studying linguistics. But before you prepare to find the 'proto' language common to all languages spoken in the world today, or dissect a brain to find out where language is stored, let us have a closer look at what research in linguistics is and how you can start to contribute to the research in our field. In this chapter, I will take the critical thinking and evaluative approach discussed in chapter 8, and explain how they can help you to start conducting your own research. In particular, I will go into detail with:

- How to come up with a research question

- Which methods to use to answer such a question

- How to collect data about language

- How to present your results

- What to do with the data to answer your question

- Research ethics.

9.1 FINDING A RESEARCH QUESTION

What to study? If you want to conduct research, you need to start by looking for something about which you want to find out more. Ideally, you start with a question of some sort. This can be straightforward, such as 'do women use language differently from men?' or 'how does a child learn to use the past tense when acquiring English as a first language?' Yet, you may also do research without a clearly defined question. For example, you may want to analyse the particular way a Spanish–English bilingual friend of yours communicates. At the onset of your study you may not know what exactly you will get out of the study. So if you wanted to put down a research question in this case, it would be rather vague, such as 'how does my bilingual friend speak?', possibly to be refined at a later stage when you have studied his language and have found a direction you may be able to explore in more detail.

In actual fact there are many different types of research, and some lend themselves more easily to clear research questions than others that are more exploratory in nature.

In order to conduct any type of research, you need to use methods suited to what you want to find out. Just like there are many different types of research, there are a number of different research methods and ways in which these can be employed. This is what we will look at in more detail in the following sections.

Exercise 9.1

Before you continue reading, try to think what you would like to find out more about, and what you could imagine doing research on. If you struggle with this, think of your surroundings: do you know anybody who uses language in a non-standard way, for example because they are not native speakers of English? Do they use special words, struggle to end a phone conversation, or speak a different dialect? Maybe you can think of a common slang expression, and want to analyse which word class it belongs to. Or maybe you suspect that your female friends speak differently from your male friends. Whatever your question is, write it down and think about how you could find an answer. Do an online search: has anything been written about this subject already? As we go through the different methods below, you can return to your ideas and see how you could tackle your question.

Once you have an idea of a research project you would like to carry out, it is important to start reading. An online search will give you some initial ideas and may come up with a number of references to read in more detail. The reading will also give you ideas as to how you could conduct your data collection and analysis. For example, you may want to replicate what others have done before you. Or you may find that it would be better to use methods that are different from what has been done before, in order to get a clearer or more balanced understanding of your field of study.

9.2 DATA

The term *data* refers to the language or information relating to language you are investigating in your study. Data can take many different formats, such as numbers, tables and graphs. One typical type of data display in linguistics is through a *corpus*, which refers to an ordered collection of language data. You can put together such a corpus yourself or you may be able to find an existing corpus that suits your needs. Once you have sufficient data – of whichever type – you can carry out a linguistic analysis, and thereby start to conduct research.

Exercise 9.2

Spend a few minutes scanning through articles in the online journal *Linguistic Discovery* (you can find the link to the journal through a simple online search) or find the linguistics books published by Language Science Press. Go through different articles and find different ways in which language data are displayed.[1]

You will, most likely, have noticed that there are many ways in which linguistic data can be displayed. When an author presents data from English, these may just be presented in the text in italics *such as this example*. You will also be familiar with this way of displaying data from the present book. When the language data are from other languages, the text (often a sentence or short chunk of text) is typically accompanied by a *translation*, often in inverted commas, and a gloss. The latter is a morpheme-by-morpheme translation, giving lexical or grammatical translations for each morpheme. For example, in the following data from Greenlandic,[2] the first line gives the language data with the morpheme boundaries indicated by hyphens (-). The final line gives the translation, marked as such in inverted commas. The middle line is the gloss, consisting of lexical translations and abbreviations of grammatical forms given in small capital letters. Again, the morpheme boundaries from the first line with the data appear in the gloss. In this way, it is easy for a reader to find out how morphemes and their translations correspond to one another. There is a common code of abbreviations and ways to display the gloss that is used by many linguists; it is called 'the Leipzig glossing rules'.[3]

(59) *Meeraq*   *angutimit*   *titarta-gaa-voq.*
    child.ABS.SG   manABL.SG   draw-PASS-3SG.IND
    'The child was drawn by the man.'

(60) *Angut*   *appamut*   *igis-sima-voq.*
    man.ABS.SG   aukALL.SG   shoot-PRF-3SG.IND
    'The man shot at an auk.'

Sometimes, the Greenlandic words need more than one English word to indicate the translation and grammatical information portrayed. For example, *meeraq* means child, but is here also indicated as singular (SG) and in a special case, the absolutive.[4]

There are many other ways in which language data can be presented. The type of data you collect, and the format you display them in, greatly depends on the research you are conducting, and is usually directly linked with the methods you employ in your research.

9.3 METHODS FOR DIFFERENT PROBLEMS

In chapter 8 we saw how diverging approaches to a topic can lead to debates in a field because researchers arrive at very different conclusions. Sometimes such differences appear because of the researchers' specific theoretical backgrounds, which may influence the ways in which they approach their research and in which they phrase their research questions. Yet, differences in findings and interpretations of research results can also arise from the methods that were used in studying a research question. For this reason, it is common practice for researchers to clarify the conditions under which their research took place, so that others can duplicate the research and – one hopes – arrive at the same or similar results. Yet, again, some types of research are more easily repeated than others. Let us have a look at an example.

Imagine we wanted to find out how English children acquire the past tense in their mother tongue. There are many possible ways to answer this question. For example, we could test 100 children of different ages on their use of past tense forms. We could also record one young child over a number of months and analyse how this child refers to past events. The number of children we study and the number of hours of language we record would have to relate to how much time, overall, we have to conduct our research. While we could record many hours of one child speaking, we would not be able to do the same for 100 children, hoping to analyse it all; unless, of course, we had a lot of help or were working with a large research team.

When analysing a specific aspect in the language use of many speakers, as in the first example above, we talk about a *quantitative study*. The second type, in which we analyse the language of one or few speakers in much closer detail, is a typical *qualitative study*. Both types of studies can help us find out about how children acquire language. Yet, the results of each will be quite different from one another: in the quantitative study we get an overview of the way a wide range of children use the past tense. If there is a clear pattern, we may assume that the same will hold for other children not tested in our research. Yet, we do not know whether our results really show how individual children acquire the past tense, nor why children acquire the past tense in just this particular way. In a qualitative study, on the other hand, we will be able to establish how one child, or a small number of children, acquire the past tense, being able to analyse the different stages of their language development. However, in this case we will not be able to make assumptions about children's acquisition of the past tense in general. Rather, our findings are restricted to this particular case study.

Conducting a number of such case studies will help us understand the mechanisms behind the acquisition process. We will learn how a child starts with individual past tense forms of very frequent verbs, then acquires regular past tense forms, in order to be able to use irregular forms later. Yet, unless we conduct a wide range of such case studies, we will not be able to make any assumptions about other children. Conducting a quantitative study, on the other hand, we will get an overview of the different stages of tense acquisition that children have reached, across a range of ages. We may find that the younger children between two and three years of age use frequent irregular and some regular forms, while those above the age of five use most past tense forms 'correctly'. We may put together statistics of the number of mistakes children make in their use of the past tense, and make assumptions about the way other children are likely to behave. Thus, in this quantitative study we will be able to gain an overview of the order and age ranges in which different forms are used. However, we do not know which mechanisms play a role in the acquisition of the past tense, and we will not gain insights into how individual children acquire these tense forms.

In some cases, it makes sense to bridge between these two approaches, conducting a *mixed methods study* that combines qualitative and quantitative approaches to the research. In the case of the acquisition of the past tense, a mixed methods approach is likely to give us the fullest picture of what is going on. This is sometimes referred to as *triangulation*, using various methods to look at the same phenomenon and thereby being able to shed light on this phenomenon from various different perspectives. Conclusions arrived at through triangulation are likely to be more reliable than those arrived at through only one type of approach. Yet, not all studies lend themselves equally to a combination of quantitative and qualitative studies.

For different research questions, there are different methods that are appropriate, and mixed methods are not always the best way to conduct a piece of research. For example, in the case of analysing your friend's bilingual language use in English and Spanish, a qualitative study would probably be most appropriate to begin with. A qualitative approach allows you to look at one person's language use in greater detail. If you decided to investigate the differences between men and women's speech, it may be more appropriate to conduct a quantitative study to begin with. For example, you could ask a number of speakers about their language use, using a questionnaire. Likewise, you could set up an experiment in which speakers have to carry out specific tasks; you could then compare the findings between the male and female participants to see if there are any differences.

A good way to test whether you have chosen the right method and whether (within this) your approach is working is to conduct a so-called *pilot study*. This is a small-scale study of what you want to do, possibly with just one or few participants spending five minutes on the task. For example, if you have put together a questionnaire (see below), you can test this with one or two speakers who may point out inconsistencies or problems you were not aware of at the time of putting together that questionnaire, such as 'I do not know what to answer here, maybe you could give further options' or the like.

Exercise 9.3

Think about your research question(s) from above. Now that you know about qualitative and quantitative studies, how would you go about finding out more about the topic you would like to study? Which of the methods would be the most appropriate? Which of the methods would take the longest, as opposed to being achievable in a shorter amount of time?

I will now go into more detail with the individual types of study you may encounter, so you may change your mind as you are progressing through the remainder of the chapter.

9.4 DIFFERENT TYPES OF DATA COLLECTION

This section is about a few typical methods of data collection used in linguistics. Some of these, such as interviews, are most typically used with qualitative studies. Others, such as experiments and questionnaires, are typically quantitative.

9.4.1 Recording spoken language data

If you want to analyse spoken language data, you may already have access to existing data, such as a TV debate or other material available online. Yet, if you want to analyse your bilingual friend's language use, or you would like to compare the language of your female and male friends in a short discussion, you have to record the data first.

It is relatively straightforward to record spoken language these days. Most smartphones and other devices have good recording facilities, and there is a myriad of apps and programs that can help you record spoken language data. The quality is, in most cases, very good, and there is often little need to find additional equipment, unless you are interested in phonetic details, or want to conduct professional linguistic data collection, in which case you may want to use professional recording equipment.[5]

In order to record your speaker or speakers, it may be a good idea to consider an environment in which you will have minimal interruptions and background noise. You may also want to ensure that the data you are collecting are appropriate for your research question. For example, your bilingual friend may speak very differently depending on the *domain* in which he uses language, which means the place, people, purpose and overall surroundings of a conversation. He may speak Spanish with his parents, unless English-speaking friends are present. If you wanted to record him speaking Spanish, you may have to leave the room during the recording, or you may ask him to carry out the recording.

Furthermore, when recording multiple speakers, it can get quite difficult to establish who is speaking and who they are addressing. The speakers may also be using non-verbal cues, such as gestures, to communicate. The best way to capture this is by using video recordings of your data.

There is, however, another consideration to make when recording speakers either on audio or video, which is the *observer's paradox*: the mere fact that speakers are recorded may make them tense up or try to speak 'more correctly'. The data you are collecting under these conditions may be very different from the data you get in natural situations. A way around this issue is to leave a lot of time for the speakers to 'warm up' and get used to being in a situation of being recorded. After a while, they may start to concentrate on other things than the camera or microphone in the room. A good way to make them forget is to use inconspicuous recording devices. This is, again, where it is useful to use a phone for recording, as the presence of a phone on a table is rather commonplace, whereas a camera set-up may be more intrusive.

Exercise 9.4

To avoid the observer's paradox, do you think it would be appropriate to record speakers without their knowledge? If you started to record something on your smartphone without the speakers realizing, surely you could get around the issue of the observer's paradox. Think about this, and outline reasons for and against this approach.

Once you have done that, think about how you would feel if you discovered that somebody was recording you without your permission. Would this change your mind with respect to your answer to the first part of this question?

I will discuss the question of whether it is a good idea to record people without their knowledge below in the section on research ethics. For now, I want to focus on what to do with the data you recorded. If you want to analyse spoken language, it is usually necessary to write down what was said. This is the process of *transcription*. You can try to do this manually, by playing the sound on your recording device and writing down what is said on your computer (this is what you did when writing down your text about 'what you had for breakfast' in chapter 2). You may agree that transcription can take a lot of time. Again, there are a number of ways in which transcription can be more efficient. There are programs that link the sound video of the transcription with the text you are writing down, such as *Transcriber* and *ELAN*. They may take a short while to get used to, but if you are going to do a lot of transcribing, they may be an investment that pays off very soon.

There are various ways in which you can transcribe language data. If you are interested in the grammatical structure of the text, you may want to ensure that everything that is uttered is written down (including hesitation markers like *uh*). You may also want to indicate a rising intonation, as this may mean that the speaker is asking a question. If you are interested in the way a discussion between different participants is built up, you may want to measure the pauses between turns, or the way in which speech of different participants overlaps.

9.4.2 Interviews and elicitation

Many qualitative studies use recorded language data, as discussed in the previous section. These can include cases where a speaker is asked to perform a verbal task, such as talking about their interests or telling a story. Sometimes it is appropriate for the linguist to interfere and to ask repeated questions, in which case the data collection turns into an interview. Interviews can be highly structured and follow a questionnaire (see below), or they can be more or less unstructured. Again, the format of the interview depends on what you would like to achieve. As with other language data discussed above, it is a good idea to record interviews in order to be able to transcribe what was said.

A special type of interview is elicitation. In this case the linguist prepares careful questions, for example about the way in which grammatical structures in a language work. Thus, if you have found out what the words for *I* and *you* are in a language and want to find out more, you may ask about *he, she* and *it*, and compare the findings with your existing data. Elicitation is often used in the grammatical description of languages. Yet, some linguists reject elicitation as a tool in the description of grammar as it can lead to unnatural data. For this reason, elicitation should ideally be backed up by natural language data.

9.4.3 Introspection and other types of qualitative data collection

You may also be able to collect data without having to record others, using introspection to evaluate your own language use. Historically, introspection was used by grammarians wanting to find out what was and wasn't possible in a language, and it is, to a degree, still used today. The advantage with introspection is that you do not need to find a speaker to interview – you can do it all at your own leisure, in your own time and place. The disadvantage, however, is that you may not be fully objective when it comes to your language use. You may think that something is fine to say in your language, whereas in reality you, or other speakers of the language, would never utter that particular expression. Using introspection alongside data collection from other speakers, however, can be very useful.

Possibly the opposite of introspection, if there is such a thing as an opposite, is careful observation. You may need to do this when there is no other option of collecting data. For example, you may not be allowed or able to record the language of people around you, but you can start to gain an overview of how language is used in the setting you are investigating by using *participant observation*, that is observing what happens around you, and later taking careful notes of your observation.

There are also other types of qualitative data collection, for example the use of picture stories to collect language materials. These overlap, to a degree, with experiments and more quantitative approaches discussed in the following sections.

9.4.4 Questionnaires

Chances are that you have filled in a questionnaire recently, maybe one for marketing research, a 'quiz' on social media, an evaluation of a service you used, or possibly even an academic questionnaire about language. Questionnaires provide straightforward ways to gain information, without the need to use long recording processes. Because questionnaires are so easy to use, you can hand them out to large numbers of participants and conduct a large-scale quantitative study. This is, of course, restricted by the number of possible participants you can gain access to, whether they want to participate or not and your own time restrictions.

Questionnaires are usually built up in such a way that they ask about general information alongside the specifics. So, you may be asked for your name, age, language background and similar, before going into further details, such as whether you use specific words associated with male or female speech if the questionnaire addresses the question of gender-specific language use.

While questionnaires are certainly popular and easy to use, they have a major drawback in presenting so-called reported language data. Imagine you were asked to fill in a questionnaire about your eating behaviour. Wanting to be seen to eat more healthily, you may say that you are eating those recommended seven fruit or veg a day. Such skewing of results may not even be malicious. You genuinely believe that you are eating a certain amount of fruit and veg. Only when you begin a detailed observation of your own eating behaviour, which includes noting down everything you eat, may you realise that your diet is not quite as healthy as you had assumed (or vice versa). Thus, information gained from questionnaires represents what people think or believe they do, but this may not always correlate with what they do in reality. When evaluating questionnaire data, we have to take this fact into account and – if we have the time – use other methods alongside questionnaires to gain further results about the issues we are researching.

9.4.5 Experiments

Language experiments are a favoured way to collect data in some subdisciplines, such as psycholinguistics. Experiments can also be useful methods in many other types of investigations. For example, you may want to figure out which colour words male and female speakers use. You could set up an experiment with pictures of the colours you are interested in, and show the pictures to each participant in turn, asking for the 'colour'. You may even want to look at your data in more detail, measuring the time it takes from participants seeing the picture to responding to your query. A late response could mean that they take longer to process the information, maybe because they are less familiar or less confident with colour terminology. Once you have done this with a number of speakers, you compare your results. If you decide to use statistics to carry out your analysis, it is advisable to have as large a number of participants as possible.

Other types of experiments include the use of picture stories, as hinted at above. These can be used as a true mix of quantitative and qualitative methods. You can use a comic strip or other collection of pictures that are appropriate for the issue you are to investigate. For example, if you want to look at how directions such as *into the house* and *out of the house* are expressed in a language, you could use drawings depicting these actions, asking your participants to tell you 'what is going on in the pictures'. By just using pictures, the language your participants use will not be influenced by any other language use in the context of the experiment. What I really like about this type of data collection is furthermore that you can collect comparable data from a wide range of speakers, which could be used to gain both qualitative and quantitative data at the same time.

9.4.6 Quantitative corpus analysis

Another way to work with data is to carry out a corpus analysis. You may be able to use tools such as *WordSmith* to search for patterns and collocations in a corpus, for example all instances of the word *inebriated* in combination with *absinth*. Going through the examples, you will get an idea of the ways in which language is used to express these concepts and in which types of sentence constructions they appear.

Corpus analysis is often used in the study of the historical development of a language, such as English. By searching old corpora, linguists have managed to establish when certain words first appeared in English, and which constructions they were used in.

9.5 OPERATIONALIZATION

Once you have found a method that is appropriate for your study, and potentially have carried out a pilot study, you can think about how to best put your chosen method(s) into practice. For this you may need a level of *operationalization*. It means that you indicate which measurements you are using in order to arrive at your findings. You may, for example, refer to specific terminology discussed in your literature review and indicate your understanding of each point in question. Operationalization makes it clear which variables you are using in your research, and how these are defined. Thus, if you analyse how your bilingual friend uses his languages in his day-to-day life, you may need to discuss different theories of bilingual behaviour in your literature review, and then operationalize these by referring to the categories you want to use in your own research and indicate clearly how you refer to each of these categories. Say, you want to look at your data in terms of *code-switching* (which is the use of two or more languages in the same conversation). Reading the literature on bilingual behaviour, you may find that there are different types of code-switching, such as *insertion* (the use of individual words from one language 'inserted' into the other) or *alternation* (the switch from one language to the other, e.g. at the sentence boundaries). You can say in your literature review and methodology that you will be looking at examples of these two types of bilingual behaviour in your data.[6] Giving examples of insertion, you can define how this category is realized in your data and how this differs from alternation in your study. This will make it possible for others to replicate your research, making your findings more reliable.

9.6 WORKING WITH DATA

Once you have collected enough data, it is time to start your analysis. It is a good idea to bring your data into some sort of order, such as a corpus of qualitative data or a table or spreadsheet of findings in a quantitative study. The way to begin your analysis, again, greatly depends on the type of study you are conducting. In either way, though, it is important to remember that you are not reinventing the wheel. There is likely to be some literature in the field you are investigating. If that is not the case, there will be literature about related fields. It is important to relate your research to existing research findings, and therefore the first step before embarking on the analysis of your data is to return to the literature to see what others have done before you.

Imagine you had collected data from your bilingual friend, recording him in a range of situations in which he spoke English and/or Spanish. You have transcribed all the data and are ready to start your analysis. At this stage it may be helpful to highlight the data for each of the languages. For example, you could highlight Spanish in capital letters, while English is kept in lower case. That way, you get a visual idea of the distribution of both languages, which may help you in structuring your analysis. You may want to divide the text up into situations where your friend speaks exclusively Spanish or English, or where he mixes his two languages. You can then examine what may cause his language choice in each situation, such as the people he is talking to, the topic he is talking about, the place of the conversation, the other people present (including you, the researcher) and so on. For situations where he mixes both languages, it might be an idea to see if there is one underlying language into which elements from the other language are inserted, and to analyse the word classes of the words in that other language. Once you have done that, you can go back to the literature on *bilingualism* and code-switching to get further ideas on how to proceed with your analysis. You can also compare your own findings to those of others: do your findings confirm what others have said, or do you get unexpected results?

Whatever the study you are conducting, it is advisable to be systematic in the way you approach your data. Yet, you may not be able to focus equally on everything that you found. Sometimes you have to make the decision to focus on just a few aspects of your data, for example when you want to present a coherent and clear study. Less is often more; an essay with a clear focus and consistent analysis of the data will be much better than an essay that looks at a wide range of random data.

It is also important to refer to different aspects of our data. For example, if we have collected quantitative data about the differences between the language use of men and women, we may have put together a spreadsheet with the results, indicating the number of 'yes' or 'no' answers for each category. It may be tempting to go through each question and list the percentages of 'yes' and 'no' encountered. Yet, in order to understand fully what is going on in the data, we have to relate our findings to the sex of the participants. We have to find out which percentage of the female speakers answered the question with 'yes', and which percentage of the male speakers answered 'yes', in order to establish whether there is a difference between the two groups. There may be a correlation in that all females do one thing, and all males another, yet this may well not be the case. Linguists tend to use *statistics* to find out if the findings are *significant*. This means there is a strong likelihood that the findings are not due to chance. To carry out a statistical analysis, many linguists use the programs SPSS or R, but it is also possible to do statistical analyses through regular spreadsheet programs like Excel.

So far, we have discussed correlating the findings for each question with the background information on whether the participants are male or female. Yet, we may want to carry out another level of analysis in correlating some of the questions. For example, a question about using a specific colour word like *mauve* may show significant differences between male and female participants, while using a colour word like *lilac* may not come up with significant differences between the two sexes. Yet, it would be interesting how the individual speakers using *lilac* relate to those using *mauve* and other colours. Is there a small group of speakers that use particularly detailed colour terminology, which may or may not be linked to whether they are male or female? Is there, perhaps, an explanation for their use of such details, for example their work background or interests? In this case, it would be good to know a little bit more about the participants in question, which needs to be considered before the actual study, at the time of putting together the questionnaire.

There is, possibly, a lot we could relate and investigate, and not all of it will be equally relevant or interesting. My students sometimes lose oversight of their data and struggle to find the relevant aspects to focus on. In this case, I usually advise them to go back and think about what they initially wanted to find out about and which part of the data could be used to answer that question. In the end, this may just be a fraction of the overall dataset.

9.7 RESEARCH ETHICS

When working with people, in this case speakers of a language, it is important to consider research *ethics*. This means that the people you are working with will not be put at a disadvantage or at risk because they have worked with you. They should be treated fairly and engage in your research willingly. Thus, if you want to record someone speaking, you need to ask their permission first, unless the speech is already publicly broadcast, such as during a public speech or on the television. The participants in your research may wish to remain anonymous, for example because contributing to your research may reflect negatively on them. They may, however, want to be acknowledged for their contribution, so it is important to ask them if their names are to be used. Sometimes the things people say may be highly sensitive, for example giving names of people or referring to illegal activities. You may need to 'anonymize' parts of the text so that the people you work with are not put at risk. You may also want to consider paying the people participating in your research, or thanking them in some other way, for example by giving them a present in return for their participation.

In some studies it can be difficult to let the participants know everything about the research before you start researching. For example, if you want to study people's attitudes towards certain dialects, you may want to do so indirectly, asking about other features from which you can learn about their underlying attitudes, rather than asking outright and getting speakers' 'desirable' replies. In these cases you can give a generic 'I am interested in your opinion about x' or 'I am interested in your language background' before conducting your research, and only later tell the participants more details about your study.

Another problem may be the observer's paradox, in which case the participants tense up because they are being recorded, which results in them not using their language naturally. If this is the case in your study, you may be able to agree that you will record your speakers 'at some time during the next two days'. You may then record them covertly, letting them know that you have just recorded them immediately afterwards. In this way, you can conduct ethical research avoiding the observer's paradox.

Ethics also mean that your participants should be able to drop out of your research at any time of the study if they wish. This could become a problem for your study, but it ensures that the data are collected in a sustainable, open and ethically correct manner.

9.8 PRESENTATION OF RESULTS AND ALTERNATIVE ANALYSES

Once you have conducted your analysis and have an overview of your findings, it is time to present them. It is always a good idea to present the results in relation to previous studies, and for this you may want to go back to some of the references from your literature review. In chapter 10 I will discuss essay writing, going into more detail with the way in which data can be presented.

Your results may be exactly what others have found before you, or you may have found something new and exciting. Either way, your findings will be able to contribute to our understanding of language. Let me explore that a bit further.

Exercise 9.5

Think about a field of study and its history and look at the 'common knowledge' at any one time, as well as the 'new scientific findings' that arose in that field. Compare these to what we know today.

Whichever field of study you were thinking about (maybe whether Earth is flat or spherical), 'common knowledge' has a tendency to be overhauled in the light of new findings. Sometimes it can take decades, or even centuries before new findings become common knowledge.

Sometimes, new findings cause a stir, especially if they go against common knowledge and established wisdoms. To argue your case forcefully, it is a good idea to show how you arrived at these unexpected findings. If you give clear indications of the methods used and the conditions under which the results were achieved, presenting the data or your corpus of data used in the study, others will be able to replicate your study and test whether they would arrive at the same results. This is important, especially when there are differences in opinion. Testing the results of others and coming up with the same findings will, in this case, strengthen the conclusions about the data. Research is not necessarily about finding out new things. In many cases, it is looking at something that has been tested before to confirm whether this is true under different conditions, or to look at an old problem in a new way. That is why research is highly linked to what has come before and should be done in conjunction with previous research in the field. There is little point in reinventing the wheel!

Research, these days, is often mentioned in the nominal compound *research impact*. This refers to the outcome of research having some 'impact' in society. Some research has clear impact, for example a cure for cancer will have a great impact. Yet, some research may not seem to have an immediate impact, but later it may turn out to be essential for something else, perhaps totally unexpected, to work. Thus, studying an indigenous language from the Amazon, you may be able to show that languages can do things that are very different from what we previously thought human languages could do. Knowing about this, people studying what is possible in languages may be able to make more detailed assumptions about how language developed overall and learn about human cognition. This research may, indeed, have a great impact.

FURTHER READING

There are a number of useful research methods books aimed at students of language and linguistics. Podesva and Sharma (2013, eds.) *Research methods in linguistics* is a collection of chapters written by experts in individual methods. Another book with the same title, also comprising chapters written by different experts in the field, is Litosseliti (2010, ed.) *Research methods in linguistics.* Dörnyei (2007) *Research methods in applied linguistics* is particularly aimed at students of applied fields, such as second-language acquisition and sociolinguistics. The book discusses qualitative, quantitative and mixed methods, including details on a range of statistical analyses. Gries (2013) *Statistics for linguistics with R* is a useful tool for those carrying out detailed statistical analyses, discussed in relation to data from the field. There are also many methods books specifically aimed at individual areas of study, such as Wodak and Meyer (2009, eds.) *Methods for critical discourse analysis.*

A good book to help you find out about different areas of study and to learn about possible research projects is Wray and Bloomer (2012) *Projects in linguistics and language studies*, 3rd edition. The authors discuss a wide range of studies that undergraduate students can carry out successfully, indicating possible methods and approaches for each.

NOTES

1   These journal articles and books are easily – and freely – accessible online. A simple online search should suffice to find these publications. If you have trouble accessing these websites, any other linguistics publication, such as a book or journal, will suffice.
2   Collected by Jeanette Sakel during fieldwork in Greenland, 1998, from Sakel (1999).
3   These are available online and can be found through a simple internet search.
4   This is a special case in Greenlandic and other so-called ergative languages, which use different case-marking systems from English and most other European languages.
5   Many linguists use 'solid-state' recorders and external microphones for this type of recording. High-quality equipment is not necessarily expensive. The best way to find out which types of equipment are available is to look at online reviews and discussions. You will want to search for equipment that receives excellent reviews specifically for recording the human voice, which has a different frequency range from music.
6   For more on types of code-switching data, see Gardner-Chloros (2009).

Assessment

Presenting your skills

IN THIS CHAPTER

In this chapter, I look at working independently and preparing for different types of assessment, with the main focus on how to do well on your course:

- Working independently

- Writing an essay or other type of coursework

- Finding references

- Giving a presentation

- Achieving a good mark in essays and exams.

10.1 WORKING INDEPENDENTLY

University study is different from school and college in that you are expected to work independently. That means you will have to manage your own time and have to find an approach to your studies that works for you. Your input will greatly shape your overall success. It can be difficult to plan all this when having a lot of (perhaps newly found) freedom.

One part of that is to keep on top of what is expected of you, and to keep up-to-date with exam and coursework dates and other requirements for the successful completion of the course.

Most universities provide course handbooks, accessible through their virtual learning environments. This is where news, lecture notes, marks and other materials are usually published as well. It is important to familiarize yourself with this learning environment and ask for help (such as by signing up to specific training courses in how to use the technology) if you are not confident in using it. As a student, you are often expected to find the relevant course information that tells you what to do to successfully complete the course. Lecturers may not always tell you all of this, and it is easy to miss out on important information. For this reason, it is a good idea to team up with others on your course to share information. Join or set up a social network group for your course, follow your course blog if there is one, and set up a *reading group*. Working independently does not, after all, mean that you have to be on your own.

Coming back to reading groups, these can be an efficient way to discuss the course content and help each other. You can, for example, get together with the same handful of students on your course each week, discussing the course content, reading and exercises. You can learn from each other, and challenge each other in the topics you have just learnt about. It is also a great environment in which to develop ideas or questions to bring up in the next session. Your lecturers are likely to be very happy to answer questions arising from such discussions, and it shows that you have been engaging with the subject content. The following are some ways in which you can do well working independently:

- Be prepared to know what is expected of you, and locate handbooks and other course information.

- Make a diary for assessment times, and plan your own learning journey. For example, plan when to start writing essays, timetable study time, free time and work time.

- Collaborate with other students, such as in a reading group or as part of a social network group of your course.

- Ask your lecturers if any aspects of the course remain unclear, or sign up for specific training courses.

Self-organization and time management are the cornerstones of a successful degree, and both are excellent skills that employers look for after you graduate. Being able to give pertinent examples of keeping to tight deadlines, for example, can impress a potential employer at a job interview.

10.2 WRITING AN ESSAY OR REPORT

Almost certainly, you will have to write an essay or report during your studies. Most universities have specific essay writing guidelines, and it is important to know these before you start writing. Yet, there are a number of general points when it comes to writing a successful essay.

The process of essay writing can be summarized as follows:

Table 10.1
The essay writing process

The question: what do you want to find out?

The literature: what has been written on this topic before? What has been written in related areas?

Read through the literature taking notes, for example what you agree or disagree with. At this stage it is also a good idea to write down the name, year and page number of each publication, so that you can get back to it again at a later stage.

Think about ways in which you can test or investigate your question in the light of what you read.

Design a study, collect data and analyse your results (if your essay involves conducting your own research).

Relate your results to other studies: what have you found out that can contribute to our understanding of language?

A good essay needs some preparation, and it is best not to leave it too late to start doing your research. If you know the essay topic in advance, you could even start early in the term with your initial planning.

You may be given a choice of essay topics or have to find your own within a certain area. If you are unsure which topic to pick, it could be a good idea to read up on the different subjects superficially first. I find it helpful to do a brief online search on each topic. Think about what you could imagine working on for the required amount of time, or whether you would get bored with a topic after a week. You may even be able to find a personal link to the topic, which could give you an extra incentive. For example, if you know a bilingual speaker of English and Polish who frequently mixes both languages when speaking with other bilinguals, why not investigate such code-switching in more detail in your essay?

From my own experience as a lecturer, it ultimately makes little difference which essay topic you pick, as all will be equally 'difficult', even if one may appear easier at first glance. Yet, the enthusiasm with which you approach a topic can greatly influence your mark. Interesting or challenging essay topics can lead to much better results than 'standard' topics done many times before. It is usually a good idea to be creative in your choice!

10.2.1 Finding references

Once you have an idea about your topic, you can start to look for literature and other information. Again, the internet can be a very useful resource for an initial overview. But be careful when selecting the right references for your essay, as online materials are not always suitable.

A university essay or report generally needs to be accompanied by references, which give evidence of the information you base your claims on. These references are official textbooks, scholarly books, journal articles or reports. They are usually peer-reviewed, which means that they have gone through a process of evaluation by other scholars. For this reason, the evidence given in these books is likely to be of higher quality than publications that have not gone through such a process (there are exceptions, of course). Many texts available online have not been peer-reviewed, and may have been written by authors who knew little or nothing about the topic they discuss. Some websites of the *wiki* type are semi-peer reviewed, in that they can be altered by experts across the world. Yet, we still cannot trust all of the information given in these sources.

Despite these shortcomings, the internet also houses a wide range of materials that can be used as references, which can, for example, be found through *Google Scholar*. Also, the search engine on your university library webpage will be a good place to look for peer-reviewed literature.

A great way into a topic is to find a few relevant and recent[1] books to begin with. Then, you can look in their list of references to find other texts that may be relevant for your study. It is important to reference a range of sources, rather than relying on just one or two texts. You may not always find many (or even any) materials on all topics, but you may be able to look at related areas of research. For example, you may be interested in how Somali native speakers acquiring English as a second language use markers of negation. It is unlikely that you will find a new textbook or even a journal article on this topic. Yet, you can look at the wider topics of second-language acquisition and negation in general, and then at how speakers of other languages (e.g. French or Chinese) acquire negation in English or other languages. You may also try to find other general literature on how speakers of Somali acquire English and other languages. Of course, should you find publications that deal specifically with your topic, it is important to read these carefully and reference them in your essay.

I have often found it helpful to take down notes while reading, indicating the name of the publication and page number alongside each note. This is so that I can easily find the text again for referencing. This also avoids accidental *plagiarism*, which means copying something directly or indirectly from others without acknowledging them. Plagiarism is viewed as a serious assessment offence at most universities, and can lead to being expelled from university.[2]

10.2.2 Writing the main body of an essay

Notes from reading the literature can be an excellent start to an essay. Rather than being faced with a blank page, you will be able to summarize findings or claims on the basis of these notes. Having picked your topic, you will also be able to describe your area of study, maybe even state your research question, if you have one. At this stage, it is a good idea to stand back and think carefully for a while before embarking on writing. Rather than writing an essay from the first word till the last (which, honestly, only very few people can do), try to write down some of your ideas: what do you think is important? What should be there?

Once you have a few points written down on paper, you can sort them into headings and put together a table of contents for your essay. There may be obvious headings such as 'introduction' and 'literature review', but you may also have more specific headings for different sections of your essay. Figure 10.1 gives an overview of typical sections of essays. Make sure that you read the guidelines for essays on your course carefully, as they could be very different.

Figure 10.1
Typical sections of an essay

- Introduction (outlining the research question)
- Literature review
- Hypothesis/research question (unless treated as part of the literature review or introduction)
- Methods (if you used research methods)
- Results (to state the results of your research without any analysis)
- Discussion (analysis of the results)
- Conclusion
- List of references
- Appendix (if you want to present further evidence relevant to the essay)

The sections of your essay will greatly depend on the type of essay you are writing, and what your course requirements are. Again, there are a number of pointers on how to achieve a good mark for an essay:

- An *introduction* is your reader's first impression of your essay, and the first overview they get of what you want to achieve. Therefore, it is important to set out what your essay is about and what the structure of your essay is. You may place this in a context of interest, e.g. former studies showing different results, an ongoing debate in the field, your own personal interest in the case studied. Yet, it is important to be very clear, not keeping your reader in the dark (remember your readers are likely to mark your essay!).

- The *research question(s)* would usually arise from the *literature review*, and appear at the end of this chapter or in a separate chapter following the literature review. That is, unless your essay is a simple review of the literature on a specific topic. In any case, it is a good idea to refer to the research question in your introduction.

- If you collect your own data, it is important that you clearly state your research *methods*, and present your *results*. Sometimes a separate section called 'results' or 'findings' follows the description of the methods. This section would usually be an overview of the main findings, while extensive data sets are best presented in the *appendix,* an optional part of the essay where you can present extra information. Usually such an appendix does not count towards the overall word count.

- The *discussion* is, in my opinion, the most important part of an essay. It is the place where the writer discusses the findings in the light of the literature set out in an earlier section. For example, you can compare your findings to those of other studies, analysing why your results are similar or different. This is the section where the overall analysis takes place, and the findings of the study are put into shape. For this reason, some people refer to this chapter as *analysis*.

- The conclusion may be just that: a summary concluding the main findings and drawing the essay to a close. There may also be an outlook for future studies.

- The list of references gives details of the literature you used in your text. There are a number of different formats that vary from course to course. It is important not to confuse a list of references with a bibliography, which lists a wide range of sources on a topic, not all of which are necessarily mentioned in the text. Indeed, bibliographies are not commonly used in academic essays. Rather, you will be expected to present a list of references that lists all of the sources mentioned in the text. As you are writing, you are expected to give the source of your information in the text, usually by listing the last name and year of publication. You should also indicate the page numbers if you refer to a specific section of the publication (e.g. Dörnyei 2007: 34–35). The list of references appears at the end of the essay and gives all the details of the publications used, ordered alphabetically by the last name of the author. The list of references at the end of this book could guide you as an example. But be aware of your own university's guidelines, as they may prefer a specific format for referencing (such as 'Harvard', 'MLA' or 'Chicago').

Once you have found a suitable format for your essay, you can start to write down some notes on what you want to write about. It is a good idea to put together a preliminary table of contents, which will guide you as you start to work on the different sections of the essay. When stuck with one section of your essay, you can always go on to a different part, or even a different essay. I find that doing something else for a while can give a new perspective on things that were difficult to resolve at first.[3]

It is worth keeping in mind that even though essays reference the literature, they are still your own contribution to the field. For this reason, it is important to distinguish between your own results and those given by others. In all cases it is important to relate your own results to the findings in the literature. For example, if your essay was primarily a review of the existing literature, make sure you present the results of what you have learnt, such as whether the researchers working in this area are in agreement or disagreement, the newest findings in the field, as well as your own perspective: what do you think about the controversy, if there is one? Why do you think one argument is more convincing than another? Can you add anything to the debate, such as your own examples?

Essays often include a section on future work. Sometimes the methods did not work satisfactorily, or the research identifies areas that are so far very little researched. This is of course relevant and ought to be mentioned. However, comments like "I could have read more recent books about this topic, which would have given me a broader perspective" should be avoided, as they will only provoke the question why you didn't read those books in the first place!

10.2.3 How to achieve a good mark in an essay

A good essay is one that is consistent and adheres to the requirements. You can write an amazing piece of work but will not achieve a good mark if it is not what you were asked to do. I sometimes see essays with very long and highly impressive literature reviews, but a rushed and insufficient discussion of the findings. The students may have run out of time, spent too long on the literature review without progressing to the rest of the study. Or they may have been too ambitious in what they could achieve. If the call is for a small-scale study, it is important to stick to this brief. Time is better spent in linking the discussion back to the literature review, and making the essay readable and clear.

In an ideal world, you have plenty of time left after finishing your essay before it needs to be handed in. This can sometimes be difficult, especially when writing more than one essay at the same time. Yet, with a bit of planning it is achievable and can greatly increase your overall mark. Preparing an essay for hand-in can involve the following steps:

- Look again at the guidelines for essay writing on your course: did you follow all instructions?

- Read through the essay carefully and look out for misunderstandings or anything that is unclear.

- Look at the overall structure of the essay: are all the relevant subjects treated appropriately?

- Does the essay answer the research question set out in the beginning?

- Read through your introduction again: have you done what you promised? Or did you say that you would look at a certain theory in greater detail but only mention it in passing later?

- Check the language and style, as well as the word-flow: does the essay read well? It sometimes takes three or more revisions to get this right. Also run a spell-check to make sure all typos are removed.

- Check the layout, avoiding headings at the bottom of the page and inserting page numbers. It is a good idea to start a new paragraph with each new thought. Using a readable font, such as Cambria 12, also helps.

- Ensure that you keep to the word limit, if there is one.

- Check that all sources mentioned in the text are given in the list of references, and that all sources in that list appear in the text.

- Try to read the essay as though someone else had written it. If you feel that you are too close to your own essay, exchange essays with a friend and truly read someone else's essay. This is a great way to give and receive feedback, and to get ideas for how else to approach an essay in the future.

10.3 GIVING PRESENTATIONS

Many students find giving presentations the most daunting aspect of their course. Most of us are not born presenters. Even your best lecturers will probably have gone through stage fright before they fully developed their lecturing skills. The following hints may help you to give successful presentations:

- Be well prepared and know what you will talk about inside out.

- Work on a clear structure for your presentation, highlighting the most important points first.

- Try to talk through the presentation a few times before the real event and work on aspects that you struggle with.

- Prepare a handout or digital presentation (using programs such as *Keynote*, *PowerPoint* or *Prezi*), which can structure your presentation and guide you as you go along.

- Time yourself and cut down on the content of your presentation if necessary. As a rule of thumb, I would allow at least two minutes per short example (or *PowerPoint* slide).

- Aim to talk slowly and clearly (which is not always easy when nervous!).

Your university may offer courses in presenting, which could be worth signing up to. Even if your first presentations do not work out too well, it is important not to despair. It takes a lot of practice to become a proficient and good presenter. The time at university could be seen as 'practice time' before it really matters. Even if giving presentations is not an obligatory aspect of your course, it is useful to keep in mind that many employers look for such skills, and having developed techniques to present well is a clear advantage in many different types of employment.

10.4 PERFORMING WELL IN EXAMS

As in the other types of assessment, performing well in exams has to do with your overall preparation. Even if you get nervous when the clock is ticking, there are a number of ways to prepare for a successful exam performance:

- Prepare by participating in classes, taking notes and asking questions when something is unclear.

- Understand the format of the exam beforehand. At many universities, you can see past exam papers. It is a good idea to work through these, provided the course has not changed substantially. You can discuss your results with other students, or ask your lecturer if they are able to look over your answers and give you feedback.

- At the beginning of the actual exam, take a few minutes to understand the questions and the exam layout. Then make a schedule for the remainder of the exam, allowing a certain amount of time for each question. This way, you won't spend too much time on one question and miss out on marks in other parts of the exam.

- As with essays, it is important to stick to the guidelines in exams. If your lecturer asks for a short paragraph, it is advisable not to write many pages on the topic. In my own experience, students can lose marks when writing too much, as there is more chance for error (in the unnecessary elaborations).

- If you can choose between questions, it is important to think carefully about which questions you may do best at, rather than answering all questions half-heartedly and missing out on vital points that way.

- Rather than starting to write straight away, it is helpful to work out the format of your answer. A well-prepared answer tends to gain more points than something scribbled in haste.

- Make sure that you answer (or at least attempt to answer) all parts of the questions, even if the answer is very brief or obvious. Not answering parts of questions inevitably affects your overall score.

- If you have the luxury of spare time at the end of the exam, go through it all again, ensuring that you have followed all of the instructions and answered all parts of the exam.

10.5 SUMMARY: HOW TO ACHIEVE GOOD MARKS

In summary, the way to do well at university has a lot to do with knowing the ways in which to achieve a good mark. Of course, the best advice is to study hard. Yet, there are also a number of other techniques that should help you do well:

- Know what you are doing: in particular, know the guidelines set out by your course. You may be able to find marking guidelines, outlining what is expected of a student achieving a certain mark.

- Be prepared by going to classes, participating and doing the required reading and exercises. If you had to miss a class or went to a class unprepared, try to make up for it by going through the lecture notes and talk to other students. Understanding new content in small chunks is easier than having to read up on it all just before the exam.

- Give it all good time, for example by starting essays early and by working to a deadline a week before the official hand-in date. That way, you will have more time to do the crucial rewriting and fine tuning that can lead to a good mark.

- Ask for feedback from your lecturers, and use this feedback to do better in the future. You may feel that once you handed something in, all you want is a mark and never hear about or see that piece of work again. And indeed, feedback can feel cruel. It takes strength to get over it and regard feedback as something positive. After all you have (ideally) spent a long time preparing for your assessment. It may help to put the feedback aside for a few days and then come back to it and reread it slowly and carefully. Spending another ten minutes or so on developing strategies for the future is a very good idea, as these ten minutes may help you save a lot of time at the next assessment, and you are much more likely to achieve a better mark in the future.

Exercise 10.1

Try to locate course-specific information for your university (or the universities you are considering for future study). Are any of the materials published online? Can you get access to recommended reading?

If you are already a student, try to put together a detailed work plan for your degree course. This could be a timetable for when to do what, thinking about topics you might want to go into further detail with during your studies and so on.

Overall, try to relate the issues discussed in this chapter to your own study situation.

FURTHER READING

A handful of books deal with essay writing in linguistics, such as Murray (2012) *Writing essays in English language and linguistics: principles, tips and strategies for undergraduates*. Wray and Bloomer's (2012) *Projects in linguistics and language studies* includes some information about essay writing and giving presentations.

There is also a wealth of generic literature on essay writing, such as Greetham (2013) *How to write better essays* and Warburton (2007) *The basics of essay writing*. Likewise, there are many generic self-help books on time management and giving presentations.

For referencing, try to find your university's specific resources. These are often located in the university library and on their website. Your university may ask you to use one particular style of referencing, such as 'Harvard', and most libraries provide information and resources for students on how to go about referencing correctly.

NOTES

1　A book published in 1934 may not necessarily show the current state of a field. That is not to say that historical books are of no value, but unless you are researching a historical topic, it is advisable to find the most recent publications in this area first to get an overview of the field.

2　In some cases it may even catch up with you years later. For example, a German government minister's PhD thesis was found to contain significant plagiarism from other studies and even newspaper articles. He had to resign and his university decided to take away his title. This case inspired a number of other PhD theses to be scrutinized, and further ministers have since had to resign because of plagiarism in their work.

3　At this stage you may start to delete things you have written. I find it useful to have a 'cut out' document, in which I collect everything I wish to delete. There have been quite a few occasions where I realized that something was useful after all, and I had a way to retrieve the information.

11

How to find out more about language

IN THIS CHAPTER

Being aware of what is required of you, initiative and collaboration can all greatly contribute to gaining good marks, as we explored in the previous chapter. Yet, the most important part of doing well is by gaining subject knowledge. There are many ways in which you will acquire such knowledge, such as by participating in lectures and seminars, reading about a topic or researching an issue in more detail. In this chapter I will look at the resources available to you to learn more about language beyond lectures, seminars and other direct learning resources available at your university:

- Researching a topic

- Terminology

- Academic publication formats

- Understanding difficult texts

- Libraries and other resources.

11.1 RESEARCHING A TOPIC

At the beginning of university study, it can be bewildering to find out about the different places where you can gain information about language. Books can be a good start, whether they are bought, accessed online or found in the university library. Sometimes you find books that deal with just what you had been looking for. In other cases you may have to look at a wide range of materials to investigate a phenomenon from different perspectives. For example, you may be interested in the way pronouns are used in the Bristolian variety of English. Most likely you will not be able to find a book that discusses this topic in detail. Rather, you will have to look for books, journal articles, book chapters or online materials discussing Bristolian, South West varieties of English, or even more general books about the different dialects across the UK. In the latter case, only a very small part of the publication may be relevant to your interests. Additionally, unless you can find information about pronoun use in Bristolian English, you may want to look for pronoun use in general, and perhaps find examples from other varieties of English. Then, you may be able to find an online video or audio extract of someone speaking Bristolian, which you can then analyse in more detail on the basis of the background knowledge gained from reading about the topics of British dialects and pronoun use. In effect, you are conducting your own research (see chapter 10).

To guide you through the maze of academic publishing, I will discuss a number of different publishing formats. Since many academic publications use subject-specific terminology, it is a good idea to gain a good overview of the terminology used in the field. For this reason, I will start this chapter with a section on how to understand – and remember – new linguistic terms you come across.

11.2 TERMINOLOGY

Publications in linguistics tend to use a lot of subject-specific terminology, and it can be overwhelming to make an inroad into some texts because of that. You could invest in a special linguistics dictionary, or you could simply use online resources to help you with the definitions. On smartphones and tablet computers, you can easily access definitions by highlighting the word you do not understand, provided you have downloaded the appropriate dictionary.

To avoid having to look up new or difficult terms all the time, you may want to consider putting together your own database of new terms. You could start with a simple list of terms and short definitions, or put together an alphabetically ordered spreadsheet. You could also set up a system of electronic flashcards, such as in *Memrise* or similar programs, where you can link a new term with a memorable picture and definition, tailored to your own learning needs. Reviewing and 'learning' new terminology pays off, and you may soon feel that you understand much more than before.

It is also a good idea to set the new terminology in context with related terms. For example, you may have learned about the *Romance Languages*, that is languages deriving from Latin, including the major languages Italian, French, Spanish, Portuguese and Romanian, as well as a range of smaller languages. While finding out what they are, you could try to find similar groupings of other language families, such as the *Germanic Languages*. Once you have understood in which way this terminology is used, you can try to contrast it with groupings such as the *European Languages*. While the latter is just a geographical notion, the languages traditionally spoken in Europe, the former two are language groups that descend from a common ancestor.[1]

11.3 TYPES OF ACADEMIC PUBLICATIONS

As you progress through your course, you will probably be asked to conduct reading of a wide range of resources, and reference this reading in your essays or reports. In this section, I will look at some of the typical types of publications you will encounter. The first type of publication you are likely to encounter on your course is a textbook. Indeed, the present book is such a textbook. Textbooks are written with specific student audiences in mind, often relating to commonly taught courses or issues many students are likely to encounter. Textbooks are often more accessible and easy to read than other academic publications, because the authors take into account the knowledge-base of their audience. Textbooks also tend to include exercises, indications for further reading and a glossary. Sometimes modules and courses are organized around specific textbooks, while at other times you may be presented with a range of informal *teaching materials*, which may have been put together by your lecturers to suit the course. Such materials include exercises, collections of important texts, or collections of examples for you to analyse.

New research findings are generally presented in *journal articles*. Since journal articles are aimed at other linguists, they are often much more difficult to understand than textbooks. Luckily they tend to start with a short *abstract,* which is an overview of the research question and findings. Reading the abstract will give you an idea as to whether the overall article – or 'paper', as academics tend to call it – is what you are looking for. Apart from the abstract, journal articles are built up in a similar way to essays (discussed in chapter 10). There are a wide range of journals in linguistics and affiliated fields, and many have specialisms in certain subfields. For example, the *International Journal of Bilingualism* mainly attracts articles dealing with the phenomenon of bilingualism, as well as from related fields such as language contact and language acquisition. There are also journals that are less specific in their fields, such as *Language,* which is one of the most highly regarded journals in the field of linguistics, and which is deliberately open to publications from the entire area of linguistics. Many papers sent to this and other high-ranking journals are rejected for publication through the process of peer review (see below), and it is a mark of great distinction to publish in this and similar journals. There are further journals such as *Nature* and *Science* which attract an even broader audience, and in which linguists are sometimes able to publish, getting a much wider distribution of their findings.

Another type of publication is a *research monograph.* This is a book about a specific topic, with the same kind of audience as journal papers. Again, compared to textbooks, research monographs are often considerably more difficult to understand, as they are aimed at an academic audience.

Some books are *edited volumes,* usually about a specific topic that all chapters have in common. They initially resemble research monographs in being books and in having an academic audience. Yet, the chapters of edited books are written by different authors. The editors of the overall volume generally contribute an introduction, and sometimes write other chapters too. You may also find that some journals publish *special editions*, which are comparable to edited volumes in that they are a collection of articles on the same topic, written by a range of academics.

You may come across a wide range of other publications, such as *research reports* aimed at particular practitioners or the general public, websites and other online materials. Depending on their audience and focus, they may be easier to understand than some of the academic publications. However, they may not be equally 'scientific' in the same way as journal articles. How, you may ask, is it possible to judge how 'trustworthy' a publication is?

While even academic publications may not be fully 'trustworthy', for example because new findings may later supersede them,[2] there is still a good mechanism ensuring a high quality and thorough methodology in academic publications through a process called *peer-review*. Peer-review means that other linguists, often anonymously, read and comment on the paper before it is considered for publication. They decide whether a book or paper is appropriate for publication, or whether it needs reworking in any way. Academic journals, academic monographs, textbooks and edited books are generally peer-reviewed, while most websites and reports are not. Hence, finding information on a topic on a web-based service such as Wikipedia may be good for an initial overview, but such material may not always be peer-reviewed.[3] When writing an essay, you are most likely required to use peer-reviewed publications in your references.

Despite not being peer-reviewed, a number of online resources can be really helpful in getting you going. I have been producing some such materials myself – e.g. short videos to introduce specific terminology and concepts in linguistics. There are also numerous blogs run by linguists (such as 'LanguageLog') or students of linguistics, which are worth exploring. As long as you keep in mind that these may not be appropriate references in essays, but rather serve as a starting point for your own learning, you can enjoy these and learn a lot that way. Some may even receive a form of 'peer-review' without necessarily stating so directly. For example, there is a lot of information on linguistics freely available through lecture capture, 'Ted talks' and other online academic resources.

Yet, there are also publications that appear to be peer-reviewed, yet are of a dubious quality. These are sometimes referred to as predatory open-access journals. While there are many good examples of high-quality open-access journals in linguistics (such as 'Linguistic Discovery') and online book publications (for example through 'Language Sciences Press'), there are also many new journals that have been established purely to allow for 'vanity publishing'. Authors pay a fee to publish their paper in such a journal. On the front, it appears that there is a process of peer-review, yet this may not always be carried out. The resulting papers are, for the most part, of a far lesser quality than what you would expect to encounter in a genuinely peer-reviewed journal.

11.4 HOW TO USE THE INFORMATION YOU FIND

If you are researching a specific topic, you may already have some publications in mind that you want to use as references (see chapter 10). If not, you could start by reading as much as you can find about the topic you are interested in. You could search for the terms you are interested in online, or search for the topic in your library database. It is a good idea to try out different search terms. Thus, when the search *Pronouns in Bristolian English* does not come back with any results, you may want to try broader searches such as *Bristolian* first, before narrowing down your search terms to achieve more specific results. Once you have found a publication that deals with the topic (even if it is just doing so marginally), you can usually find references to other publications that are appropriate for your research. Going through the lists of references of publications can be a good way to find information otherwise not accessible or difficult to find. Just remember that the references will be older than the original, so if you start with a journal article from the 1960s, you will struggle to find reference to up-to-date research that way. You could, however, search for texts that cite these older references on 'Google scholar', which could give you up-to-date information. It may also be a good idea to find a new textbook in your general area of interest and look for appropriate references therein. Not only will it be more accessible to read, but it is also likely to give you the most important references in that particular area, which you can use as a point of departure.

If you start by finding web resources on certain topics, such as Wikipedia, you can see if they list references to peer-reviewed publications, which you can then try to find in your university library.

Another way to find information about specific topics is to go through journals dealing with your area of interest. If you want to know more about bilingualism in general, it may be a good idea to look at the newest volumes of journals such as *International Journal of Bilingualism* or *Bilingualism: Language and Cognition*. Your university library is likely to have access to these in paper or online, or you can request an 'inter-library loan' through your university librarian. This means you will be able to borrow the journal or book you require from a different library, via your home library.

11.5 UNDERSTANDING DIFFICULT TEXTS

You may want or have to read a very difficult text with a lot of new and complex terminology. It can be quite disruptive to have to look up a word in every sentence, which may refer to complex concepts or theories that take longer to understand than through reading a simple definition. Yet, there is still a way in which you can approach such a text and still access the information you are interested in, for example if that text is in exactly the right area of research you want to include in your essay.

There are a number of ways gradually to understand a text. For example, academic journal articles are usually accompanied by so-called *abstracts*. Abstracts are short summaries at the beginning of a paper, giving the main points of that paper, which include the research question(s) and the results. There are usually also notes on the methods, the reasoning for carrying out the study and how it links with other studies. Thus, reading an abstract and understanding it first is a good way to see whether the study is relevant to what you are looking at. If it looks relevant, why not proceed to read the rest of the study? You may want to read the text twice, for different purposes: first to understand the details, and to look up (and note down) new terminology, and second to reread the article in order to understand the overall line of argumentation.

If the text you are trying to read does not have an abstract, you may find some points in the introduction that can help you to see where the article is leading. You could also look at the conclusion first, but this may be less helpful. While conclusions summarize some of the findings, they may take other issues treated in the paper for granted and do not always recap the main points crucial to understanding the study (see also chapter 10 on writing conclusions to essays).

Another helpful way to gain access to difficult papers and articles is to see what others have written about the study. Try to search for others citing this particular reference (you can do so in 'Google Scholar', for example). If others have cited the publication in their literature review, they may have contrasted it with other studies or given further information crucial to understanding the reference. While this approach can be a good way to understanding difficult texts, it should also be treated with care: first of all, the information you will get is the particular author's perspective on the topic, which does not always mean the author is right.[4] The author may even be pursuing a specific agenda, or look at the topic from a very different perspective to your own (see also chapter 8).

If you have tried all these tips and still find a publication inaccessible, it is absolutely fine to decide to give up or leave it for a later date.

11.6 LIBRARIES AND OTHER RESOURCES AT YOUR UNIVERSITY

Libraries used to be places with shelves stacked full of books – row after row, right? Sure, there may be some of that still, but libraries have certainly developed into something else. At most universities libraries are spaces for study and collaborative activities. And – yes – they are also places that have something to do with books in the very widest sense. Many 'books' these days are accessible online, and rather than using stacks of files and good luck to locate what you are looking for, modern libraries have very helpful access to online databases – sometimes with direct links to the materials you are looking for.

They may be organized in such a way that study materials for linguistics are collected together in a page that you can explore – for example a link to the *OED*, a link to common study materials, maybe lecture notes, previous exam papers, links to broadcasts that deal with linguistics, etc. Whatever it offers, it is a really good idea to familiarize yourself with your university library to find out what is possible.

Libraries tend to run library induction courses at the beginning of the term, and often even throughout the year. If you struggle to find information about this, why not just go to the library and ask?

Libraries also take it upon themselves to promote study skills: they will probably have webpages showing you how to reference correctly (which system to use), how to use time management, etc., and may even offer courses to do with this.

11.7 HOW TO EXPAND YOUR RANGE OF EXPERTISE

Arguably the best way to learn more about a topic is to start reading about aspects you are interested in, which may lead you on to something else, and then something else again. Whether that reading is initially in the form of books, social network feeds, blogs or even through video or podcast resources should not matter too much as long as you feel comfortable with the format. The more you learn, the more easily accessible will other formats (for example academic publications) become.

Once you have an overview of a topic and have learnt the basics, it is still a good idea to pursue what you find interesting. If your heart is in it, you are likely to be more engaged in a topic, spend longer reading about it and learn more overall. Engaging in detail with a topic is a perfect way to learn more. Also discussions with others – be it in person or online – can really help you to understand a topic in more detail. At some point, you may start to have your own thoughts about a topic and develop your own hypotheses. You start to become a researcher, thinking about how you could confirm or disprove your hypotheses, and if it is feasible, how you could try to set up a small-scale study on the topic.

Once you have learnt something about a topic it is a good idea to share your ideas with others. I always encourage my students to write blog posts already at an early stage on the *Lingo* blog I run in collaboration with them. You may have a similar blog at your university, or you could set up your own blog site, perhaps getting together with other students to build up a website for students to publish their ideas. You could contribute to the wide variety of online discussion forums, go to undergraduate linguistics and language conferences or even publish your findings in an undergraduate journal.

Another good way to learn more and become more confident at using what you know is to relate what you have learnt to your everyday life. For example, if you work in a bar you could see how customers communicate with you and analyse your own discourse strategies. You could evaluate your own language learning success, trying to find out what motivates you to learn another language. You could carry out a grammatical analysis of a sentence written on a cereal box as you eat your breakfast. The options for using your linguistics skills are many and diverse.

FURTHER READING

If you want to learn more about the terminology used in linguistics, you may want to have a look at specific dictionaries of linguistics terminology, such as Matthews (2014) *The concise Oxford dictionary of linguistics*. Also an encyclopaedia such as Malmkjaer (2013, ed.) *The Routledge linguistics encyclopedia* can be a useful resource to learn more about terminology and different fields of study within linguistics.

You can also have a look at online Wiki websites, such as *Glottopedia*, which is specifically set up for linguistics topics.

To find out about different types of publications, it is a good idea to go to your university library or bookshop and have a look at a range of books on the linguistics shelf. Are those textbooks, academic monographs or edited volumes? Have a look online to get access to journals in the field. Many libraries list journals suitable for each area of study, but you can also ask a librarian to help you find the relevant linguistics journals to which your library has access. Try to find those journals that sound interesting to you, and read some of the abstracts and research papers. The best way to find out about the different types of publications is by using them and reading them. First, it is fine to stick to textbooks (and indeed, most of the further reading recommendations I give here are textbooks and other accessible resources). Journal articles may pose more of a challenge, and it may help to know that even seasoned linguists sometimes struggle to read articles in a different subdiscipline of linguistics.

NOTES

1   Such family relationships between languages can be seen in shared vocabulary and partially grammar, as well as regular changes to the sound in the history of these languages. Yet, even languages that are unrelated may share a lot of vocabulary and even grammar if they are or have been in contact (for example through widespread bilingualism among the speakers). For example, Finnish has many loanwords from Swedish, despite the languages belonging to entirely different families. Swedish is a Germanic language, while Finnish belongs to the Uralic language family.

2   Sometimes research results are found to be based on inappropriate research or plagiarized and the papers that have already been published are retracted.

3   At least, websites do not count as peer-reviewed in the strict sense, while the overall process of Wiki websites can, in effect, lead to highly rigorous peer-review in that various experts in the field collaborate on entries, with the history of each entry visible.

4   Sometimes people use such summaries as shortcuts, presenting the contents that others have put together, including the errors therein. It is important to research all of the aspects discussed yourself, in order to avoid plagiarism.

12

Careers

What to do with linguistics and how to get a job

IN THIS CHAPTER

Something many students are worried about is whether they will be able to have a career upon graduating. I will look at the prospects of linguistics graduates, discussing the skills gained during the degree and how these can be employed in different careers. I also look in more detail at typical careers of linguistics graduates and how you can best prepare for the world of work, write a CV and prepare for a job interview. The following topics will be discussed:

- Possible careers for linguistics graduates

- Skills gained during the study of linguistics

- How to prepare for a career

- Writing a CV and preparing for a job interview

- What you can do during your undergraduate degree to put yourself at an advantage over other graduates.

12.1 TYPICAL CAREERS OF LINGUISTICS GRADUATES

When I was choosing my degree course, my parents were unsure whether linguistics really was a good choice, asking what I would do afterwards. They felt marginally reassured when I chose German and Music as secondary subjects, thinking that I could always become a teacher if all else failed.

This attitude still persists, and you may have had similar experiences. Yet, reality is rather different from such perceptions. The answer to 'what will you do afterwards' is in short likely to be 'a great, fulfilling job' (see figure 12.1). The original attitude that there is not much employment in linguistics stems from the fact that it is not a vocational subject, i.e. a subject which leads to one specific career. When studying architecture, you can be quite certain that you will work in the area of architecture after your degree (if, that is, you can find employment). Studying linguistics does not lead to a career in just one specific area. Rather, linguistics students gain a wide set of highly desirable skills that lead to excellent chances to get a job, in a wide range of careers. If you want to keep your options open, you can try out different types of employment throughout your degree course, making up your mind in which direction you want to go upon graduation, or even changing your mind at a later stage.

The following list has been put together by Craig Evans, a student of mine, outlining some of the careers graduates with a linguistics background are pursuing:

Figure 12.1
Typical careers for linguistics graduates

Advertising account executive, advertising copywriter, archivist, bid/grant writer, computational linguist, copy-editor, data annotator, diplomatic service policy officer, editor, editorial assistant, EFL/ESL teacher, forensic linguist, information officer, interpreter, journalist, lecturer, lexicographer, magazine features editor, market researcher, marketing executive, media relations manager, political speech writer, proofreader, public librarian, public relations officer, radio producer, secondary school teacher, social media manager, social researcher, speech analyst, speech and language therapist, technical writer, trademark attorney, translator, web content writer

During your time at university, it is a good idea to give some of those careers a try. For example, you can attend careers fairs, research what a career involves and what prerequisites there are to succeed. You could carry out work experience in the area and talk to people who are working in those careers. This way you can find out whether this is really something you would like to pursue further.

It is a great advantage to have some work experience, even if this is ultimately in a different field from your chosen career trajectory. Being able to relate to your own work experience in application letters and job interviews, you can give specific examples of your experiences and show that you can, for example, tackle any issues that commonly arise in a work situation.

For some career choices it is highly advisable to have such work experience within that particular field in order to succeed. I will look in more detail at some of these below. In the next section, however, I focus on the skills you would typically gain during a linguistics and language degree, and how these are relevant to the workplace.

12.2 GENERIC SKILLS FOR CAREERS

At this stage, it is a good idea to look back at chapter 1 (in particular sections 1.3 and 1.6) and think about the skills you have gained or are intending to gain during a linguistics degree. Both the subject-specific skills as well as the transferable skills are important in preparing you for the world of employment. There have been some reports that employers look for 'soft' skills in new graduates, rather than detailed technical skills.[1] Such technical skills are usually something that graduates eventually acquire on the job, perhaps by being sent on specific training courses. Transferable 'soft' skills are often perceived as personality traits and more difficult to train, such as being good at communicating, possessing analytical and critical thinking, as well as presentation and teamworking skills. If a candidate can give examples of acquiring and using such skills during their degree, they may stand better chances at finding employment.

Yet, you may ask how you show that you are good at teamworking or analytical tasks. I find it is a good idea to start with your experience so far, and think of clear examples where you used those skills. Those may be situations where something did not go to plan and where you can show that, by acquiring or using the skills in question, you managed to succeed.

An example of how you improved could be the following. Imagine you are not particularly good at timekeeping, and realize in your first year of study that the deadlines are all too close together and you do not cope as well as you should. This is reflected in your marks, which you are certain could have been much better. You learn from the experience and make a detailed work plan for the coming year of study, dividing up your time so that you can work to the deadlines on the course. This succeeds and the evidence is that your marks improve considerably. You have now acquired a new skill, namely working to deadlines and timekeeping by planning ahead.

When giving examples such as the one above, it does not matter much that things did not go to plan at first. Rather, you are demonstrating that you can learn from failure and can solve problems, giving evidence of your success. This example does not only show your new timekeeping skills, but also highlights your willingness to improve, problem-solve and to succeed. These are desirable attributes for an employer who may need someone to be flexible, learn from their past mistakes and move on with their work in a successful manner.

Exercise 12.1

Can you think of ways in which you improved your transferable skills? Is there anything you are not particularly good at? How could you improve and turn your weakness into a positive? Alternatively, is there anything you struggled with in the past that you have learnt since?

In my opinion, you will be at an advantage as a linguistics graduate, since many of the transferable or soft skills are issues that either relate to the field of linguistics in some way (through language use) or are tasks that quite naturally form part of the linguistics education.

For example, communication skills may be acquired through the different types of assessment, such as writing essays and giving presentations. Yet, at the same time by learning more about discourse analysis, you will be in a position to analyse communication, to see where communication can break down and to develop ways to improve communication in different settings. Thus, you do not just acquire a practical skill, but you are also able to reflect upon that skill and to use this reflection to further[2] improve your ability to communicate effectively.

Typical transferable skills you acquire during a linguistics degree include:

- working independently, including timekeeping and sticking to deadlines
- working in teams to achieve a common goal
- communicating efficiently, such as when writing essays, expressing a coherent thought.

You will also develop further generic intellectual skills, such as:

- abstracting and processing information
- forming arguments, and evaluating others' arguments
- independent and critical thinking
- data analysis and respect for evidence
- problem-solving and confidence in approaching and understanding new systems.

Another skill that is important is *networking*. If you are a very social person, this may be natural for you. If you are shy, it is important to develop networking skills. Networks and links with lecturers, students and professionals could help you find your dream job. You may not always be aware of opportunities that arise, and your network may be able to point these out to you. An employer may think of you when they write a job description for a new post, if they know you are looking for a position in that area. There are a number of professional networks online (such as LinkedIn). I find it also important to keep in personal or email contact.

12.3 SKILLS AND PREPARATION FOR SPECIFIC CAREERS

So far I've looked at transferable skills and ways in which you can present yourself to a potential employer. Developing these skills is a good way to prepare for the time after graduation. If you already have a vague idea of which career path you would like to pursue, you may even be able to prepare yourself further during your studies. Some types of employment require that you have working experience in the area, or that you possess specific technical skills. While these may not be essential, possessing such experience or skills may put you at an advantage over other candidates that do not have the same level of experience as you.

The following section is based on some of my students' experiences in preparing for their careers.

12.3.1 Speech and language therapy

A handful of my students each year decide to continue on to a postgraduate course in speech and language therapy. In the UK there are only a few such courses that are funded, and there is fierce competition among applicants. The successful applicants usually have some work experience in the field. This may be through volunteering in a speech and language therapy unit or stroke centre, by supporting individual patients, or by conducting undergraduate research into an area of speech and language therapy. In order to gain this experience, it is important to start early, ideally already during or after the first year of an undergraduate degree course.

While you may aim to start working in a speech and language therapy unit straight away, it is often easiest to start by volunteering in an accessible position, such as working as a language partner in a social group for stroke victims. Thereby you develop the experience you may need in order to gain another volunteering or part-time position. You can find information about such volunteering positions through your university's volunteering or careers office. You may also find further information through a general search online.

If you discover during this process that speech and language therapy is not the right choice of employment for you, the experiences you gained during this time will still be highly valuable. You can demonstrate to possible employers that you are hard-working and have experience in working with people. You may be able to give examples of using your linguistics skills to help patients or discuss issues around patient confidentiality, which may be transferable to other types of jobs.

12.3.2 Teacher training

Another career that a fair number of my students choose is to go through teacher training in order to become a school teacher. There are different ways of becoming a teacher. Traditionally, students would study for a PGCE (postgraduate certificate in education), yet you may be able to follow another path. The best way is to look at the UCAS website to find out about the most recent requirements.

In some cases, you may be required to take an additional short course, such as a subject knowledge enhancement course, in order to be accepted on to a teacher training programme. Apart from specific academic requirements (such as a degree), you may also be asked to present additional, non-academic prerequisites. These could be some classroom experience as a teaching assistant or a certificate of medical fitness.

As with other careers, it is a good idea to try out teaching to see whether it really is for you. This way you can gain valuable practical experience, as well as try out a job before having committed to it fully. Again, it is unlikely that you will be offered a teaching assistant position at a school straight away without prior experience, but you can try to teach in other ways. You can check if your university offers PAL (peer assisted learning). In this scheme, students teach other students of the year below. PAL may be attached to specific courses or may be linked to library skills, study skills, or working with international or disabled students. In all cases, it can give you valuable teaching experience and skills in working with others. You will also gain confidence in teaching others, and possibly learn the skills you are teaching to a much deeper level than ever before. Another way to gain teaching experience is to give private lessons in a topic you know something about, for example teaching English to an international student. You can also see if your university's volunteer or careers office offers volunteering positions in school projects, which may link with teaching.

12.3.3 Teaching English (at home and abroad)

One particular type of teaching that is popular amongst students of linguistics and languages is *TESOL* (Teachers of English to Speakers of Other Languages). Through TESOL, you can travel the world and teach English for a year or even longer. Many students also build a career teaching English at home or abroad.

In order to teach TESOL, you may be required to show that you have the appropriate training, for example by studying for a CELTA (Certificate in teaching English to speakers of other languages). This usually only takes a few weeks, and most students report it to be straightforward with a background in linguistics. As with other possible careers, it may be advisable to work with speakers of other languages during your degree to get an understanding of the work as a TESOL teacher. There are even opportunities for undergraduate students to go overseas to teach English over the summer with all expenses paid. This may prove a valuable introduction to the field of teaching and you can see whether this is something you could imagine doing in the future.

12.3.4 Copywriting, editing, journalism and marketing

There are many different careers in the wider field of writing, be it as an editor, a copy-writer, a journalist, a marketing specialist or any other career associated with these. If you are considering a career in writing, it is a good idea to start writing for a number of outlets during your degree. Most universities have student newspapers, where you can work as a journalist or editor. You may have to start off as a proofreader, but once you have shown that you are serious about the task, you will be likely to be given more advanced duties. Likewise you may be able to build up your own blog or write for a student blog in your department, or work for your university's student radio. There may be student associations bringing together others interested in writing, and you may be able to publish short stories or something similar in student journals.

Yet, not just student-led outlets are open to you. Some of my students have successfully published articles in professional newspapers and magazines on a freelance basis. Often it is just a case of sending a piece of writing in for review. If the answer is 'no', it may pay off to ask for feedback and enquire how you could contribute to the outlet in the future.

12.3.5 Entrepreneurism

Not just business graduates have entrepreneurial qualities. You may have an idea for setting up your own company, and your undergraduate years could be the perfect time to test the waters. You could join an entrepreneurial society or student association, or take part in entrepreneurial competitions and ideas workshops. Some universities provide start-up funding for their students to try out new initiatives.

Typical entrepreneurial activities of linguistics graduates include setting up a language school or a language consultancy.

12.3.6 An academic career

Another path chosen by some graduates is an academic career. You may have an inkling for finding out more about a certain topic. You may really enjoy writing essays or researching specific issues. If you are considering an academic career, the best way forward is to talk to your lecturers and ask their advice. You may be able to gain an internship or funding in your department to shadow your lecturers, proofread PhD theses, contribute to teaching preparations or take part in research projects. Once your lecturers know that you are interested in the field, they may point out opportunities to you, such as undergraduate conferences, journals, project funding, funding for MA and PhD courses and more.

If you are unsure whether an academic career is for you, there is always the possibility to go back to university to study for a MA or PhD at a later stage. In my opinion, it is never too late to follow an academic route. Some of my former students came back to study for their PhDs years after they graduated. Others decided to pursue a part-time PhD alongside teaching English as their main profession.

12.3.7 Other careers

The majority of graduates in linguistics pursue careers other than those discussed so far. That is because linguistics graduates have a wide range of skills applicable in many different areas. There is no reason to panic if you do not know what trajectory you would like to follow.

For example, a student of mine could not decide what she wanted to do after graduation. Through the university careers service she gained a graduate internship at a company offering careers advice to young adults. After a few weeks as in intern, proving her worth, she was offered a full time graduate position in careers advice at the same company. Despite not knowing what she wanted to do upon graduation, she had been very active during her degree, volunteering, being a student ambassador at open days, volunteering as a student representative, working with the student union and taking on occasional work when other opportunities arose. During the interview for her internship, she could show that she had engaged with the world of work and had gained many valuable skills. She had also built up a large network of professional contacts that would become important at a later stage when she decided to study for a postgraduate certificate in careers consultancy and started to work as a careers consultant in higher education.

Exercise 12.2

Think about careers you find appealing. Next, find job announcements for such positions, learning about the skills required to be able to work in your field of interest. Try to match your own skills to those required from the applicants. Then consider ways in which you could prepare for a career in this area.

12.4 PREPARING FOR LIFE AFTER GRADUATION

In conclusion, the best way to prepare for the future is to follow your interests and combine this with building your skills base. If you are interested in learning languages, you can pursue that trajectory and it may help you to find employment in an area where language skills are necessary. If you are interested in teaching, you may want to give that a try during your undergraduate years to see if you could imagine pursuing a career in this area upon graduation. A good first step to gain new skills, as well as meeting new people and building up confidence, is to become a student representative on your course. You will serve on student–lecturer committees, bringing any issues with the course forward after discussing these with the other students on the course. If your university offers employment for students, such as during open days, it is another good way to gain valuable skills and to engage with other students and your lecturers on a different level.

12.5 WRITING A CV

A CV, short for curriculum vitae, gives information about your life. A CV is ideally a constantly changing beast that is being added to as you gain new experiences and qualifications. It also changes in being adjusted to what it is needed for. Thus, when an employer asks for candidates to submit their CV as part of the application process, the candidate would be expected to adjust the CV to the position.

Exercise 12.3

To evaluate your own CV it is a good idea to put yourself in an employer's shoes: you are going to hire a new marketing assistant. You have received three CVs of candidates who all seem to be equally qualified. The first of the CVs is 20 pages long and contains long paragraphs describing the candidate's work experience in great detail. The second CV is concise (two pages long), listing the main achievements of the candidate. The third CV, likewise, is concise. It lists the candidate's qualifications, as well as presenting a number of bullet points on how the candidate fits the role of a marketing assistant, perhaps drawing on relevant experience. Now think about which of these candidates you would prefer to meet.

Next, try to think how your own CV would appeal to an employer in the same situation.

In the exercise above, the employer would most likely invite all applicants to interview if only three people applied. Yet, often such positions attract many more applications, and a good CV will make it more likely that you will be invited to an interview.

You may think that the answer to the question in the exercise is obvious, but CVs can be surprisingly difficult to get right. While you may have a lot to say, it is important to be concise. The employer is likely to have to look at many different CVs and will be searching for information on how a candidate best fits the advertised role. You can present your skills in the best possible way by knowing about the employer and being able to relate to what your role would be should you be offered the job. If you present yourself in such a way that you focus on the achievements relevant to the role, while downplaying or leaving out less relevant information, the employer will be able to judge your skill base against the needs for the job. Provided your experience is appropriate for the task, you are more likely to be invited to interview than if you had not targeted your CV towards the job description given.

Sometimes job ads include a section outlining the profile of the ideal candidate. It is important to read this part carefully and to highlight in your CV or application form how you would fit that description.

12.6 PREPARING FOR A JOB INTERVIEW

If you are invited for an interview, it is important to find out as much as possible about the employer and the role you would be filling. You can also prepare for the interview by anticipating some of the questions you will be asked. For example, interviews often start with a question such as *Why did you apply for this role with us?* You can prepare a concise and clear answer to this, linking to your previous experience and career aspirations. For example, if you are invited to the interview for the marketing job in the above example, you may say that you are interested in a career in marketing and have prepared for this career in a number of ways (giving examples of extracurricular activities during your degree). Then you can proceed to how these skills could be used in the advertised position. It is usually not a good idea to flatter the employer too much, as in *I think this company is fantastic.* Such a statement may actually show that you know very little about the company. Rather, it is better to link some of your qualities with the services offered by the company, showing that you have thought about how you could carry out the role and that you have researched the company in more detail.

The interview is the place to show off your skills and present yourself in a good light. For this, it is important that you know which (relevant) skills you have gained. Read the job description carefully, as the employer usually lists the skills and attributes they expect of you. If you can show how you possess each of these with a clear and relevant example, you are doing well. But do not despair: even if you do not have experience in all of the points listed, you may still be able to show how you have started to learn about something, or show willingness to engage with the task should you be offered the position.

FURTHER READING

There are many resources for CV writing and preparing for job interviews. You can choose between generic materials for all types of employment, or those that are written specifically for graduates, such as Rook (2013) *The graduate career guidebook.*

There are also many guides to specific careers, such a journalism, teaching, marketing and academic positions. For a guide to postgraduate studies in linguistics, see Macaulay (2006) *Surviving linguistics: a guide for graduate students,* which goes into detail with postgraduate study in the field for those who want to pursue an academic career.

Much information about current employment projects, requirements and so on can be found online. The Higher Education Academy (HEA) regularly publishes resources and studies on employment prospects of humanities graduates. Together with a colleague, I have written such a report, which can be downloaded from the HEA website: Treffers-Daller and Sakel (2010) *Wider perspectives and more options for English language and linguistics students.*

You can read up on the skills you would typically gain during a linguistics degree by looking at the linguistics and languages benchmark statement, which is accessible online and can be found by searching for 'linguistics benchmark statement'.

A valuable resource to learn about possible careers and preparations for these are blog posts and other online resources provided by graduates. For example, on the *Lingo* blog I run with my students, a number of graduates explain how they got into studying speech and language therapy, teaching, or other positions.

NOTES

1   For example reported on the BBC; http://www.bbc.co.uk/news/education-28560758 [accessed 5.8.2014], based on a Kaplan survey of employers.
2   Note my use of a split infinitive in this sentence (as well as in a number of examples earlier on).

13

Personal development

IN THIS CHAPTER

In this final chapter I will discuss how some of the topics dealt with throughout the book can be taken one step further, asking what *you* can get out of the study of language and how the study of language can help your personal (and not just professional) development. You may wonder what exactly is meant by personal development. Indeed, it is not totally separable from the other skills discussed. Yet, studying language will give you insights that will be useful, challenging or interesting in your personal life. In this chapter, I will look at how you will be equipped to:

- Reflect on your own and on others' language use

- Evaluate common attitudes to language, and challenge those attitudes where appropriate

- Improve your writing, spelling, and general understanding of language, knowing what is important in which settings

- Being able to reflect on English in relation to other languages of the world

- Being able to approach new tasks, such as learning a language.

13.1 REFLECTING ON YOUR OWN LANGUAGE USE

Do you speak a non-standard variety of English? You may do, without necessarily perceiving your way of speaking as different from that of others.

For example, when a friend of mine originally from Manchester talked to one of my West Country neighbours, they initially struggled to understand each other, despite both speaking British English. My neighbour, speaking in a broad West Country accent, highlighted the 'strong Northern dialect' of my friend, who in return made fun of the Bristolian accent. In reality, both were speaking more or less equally non-standard varieties of English, but perceived their language to be the 'normal' variety, as opposed to the way the other spoke.

Knowing about linguistics, which includes the structures of sounds, meaning, grammar and discourse, you are equipped to evaluate non-standard language use. What is it in the language that makes it stand out as different? Which features distinguish a Bristolian accent from a Northern accent, and how does that relate to a perceived standard by each of the speakers? Is it merely the pronunciation, the words used, or are there differences in the grammar between the varieties?

You will also be able to reflect on your own language use, such as in situations where you adjust your language to different circumstances. You will, for example, be able to evaluate what it is in the way you speak to your friends that is different from the way you speak in a highly formal situation.

Once you have gained an understanding of this, it becomes straightforward to evaluate other people's language use. For example, people's social aspirations are often clearly reflected in the way they speak. Do they use manager-talk about *going forward* and the like, or do they deliberately use slang words in formal situations?

Exercise 13.1

Over the next day, try to listen out for the way in which the people around you use their language. Are there any non-standard features? Is anybody speaking deliberately formally or informally in particular situations and so on?

13.2 EVALUATING AND CHALLENGING ATTITUDES

We saw above that speakers can have the attitude that their language use is 'normal', while others are speaking varieties that render them 'wrong', 'uneducated', 'posh' or different in some other way. Another common attitude that is the subject of endless blog posts, newspaper columns and discussions is 'the decline of the English language'. Indeed, it is not just English that is – supposedly – deteriorating. Similar discussions exist in France, Germany, Denmark, indeed, pretty much everywhere that language is standardized in some way. Interestingly, such discussions have been around for a long time, and are not just developments in modern times.

Knowing about linguistics, we understand that language is constantly changing. There is variation among speakers of different generations. Language contact, as well as internal changes in a language, can lead to somewhat different structures, meanings and forms from the ones that existed before. Comparing Old English with Modern English shows how radically a language can change within a thousand years. I reckon that most speakers of English today would struggle to understand Old English.

When you are confronted with attitudes about linguistic decline, you can choose to challenge such attitudes knowledgeably, arguing that language is in constant flux and that this is a natural development. Yet, you may find these attitudes reflect a degree of conservatism and traditionalism, which the speaker may justify by presenting other examples that have nothing to do with language.

I have even come across linguists who feel torn between their personal beliefs and their academic knowledge. Someone may agree that the state of the language is 'poor' in relation to how they would prefer the language to be. However, at the same time they understand why they think this way and will know the reason for such changes (whether they 'approve' of them or not).

Awareness of such differences between personal perceptions and subject knowledge can help you change your attitudes over time, or at least understand why you react in a specific way. I know from experience that I have different attitudes towards local varieties of German, my native language. When meeting somebody who speaks with the regional accent of a variety I have negative associations with, I tend to remind myself to try to get to know the person first, before passing any (negative) judgements about them because of their language use alone. Confronting my negative attitudes by understanding why these arise has helped me to become more tolerant towards others.

Language is one of the ways in which speakers present themselves, similar to looks, displays of power and the like. Not just dialects and local accents can attract certain attitudes. For example, a learner speaking a simple and non-standard variety of their second language may be at a disadvantage over native speakers, as low proficiency in a language may be linked with negative attributes such as 'less intelligent'.

Sometimes second-language learners use words or constructions that make it difficult for native speakers to understand what they are trying to say. Having knowledge of linguistics, you may be able to evaluate how the communication failed in those instances. For example, the speaker may try to model something on their native language (a so-called *calque*), or they may be using a non-standard pronunciation which, once you have figured out how it came about, may be less difficult to understand.

13.3 STYLE

As we speak, we adjust our style to the situations we are in, taking into account the people we speak to, the place we are at, the time and formality of the event and the topic we are speaking about. These are a lot of variables, and sometimes speakers get the style slightly wrong.

Knowledge of linguistics can, again, help you to evaluate your own language use and understand how you can improve the way you communicate. Imagine you are preparing a speech for a wedding. As you prepare for the speech, you could record yourself orating and evaluate your language use. You may be using specific discourse markers (fillers) such as *uh* or *so* a lot, without realizing it while you are speaking. Being trained in linguistics, you can devise discourse strategies and adjust your language to the situation, evaluating your intonation, use of vocabulary, grammatical constructions, cohesion and coherence in the text and so much more. Most importantly, you will be able to evaluate your style to ensure that – one hopes – you are getting the tone just right for the occasion.

It is easy to get the style wrong in certain situations. Perhaps you are unaware of the conventions in a certain situation, or you are tired and have lost concentration. Sometimes your nerves can get the better of you, resulting in inappropriate language use in certain situations. I have experienced this in job interviews, where candidates lost their nerves and used informal language in an otherwise highly formal situation.

But, does it really matter? Didn't we just learn that linguists look at language descriptively, investigating how language is used rather than working to certain rules? Indeed, this is the case, yet there are situations where it is advantageous for us to know those rules and to adhere to them. While we could make a theoretical point for spelling not mattering as such, it being a secondary aspect of language use, we may need to use correct spelling in some situations. In informal situations, such as a Facebook status update, we may be creative with our spelling and perhaps not mind too much if there is a typo in the text. This depends on your personal preferences. Speaking for myself, I do not tend to mind this too much. In a job application, however, it is a good idea to use a formal style, adhering to the prescriptive rules of spelling and grammar in the language. We have learnt that the rule against using a split infinitive is a curious relic from Latin, yet an employer may react differently to you using such a construction in a formal letter. Awareness of other speakers' perceptions of language, as well as your own, can help you in choosing the appropriate style.

Also native speakers of English can attract negative attitudes if they use the wrong code in the wrong situation. Thus, using a very informal type of language in a formal situation may attract negative attitudes. This even exists in writing: using 'txt style' abbreviations in language can lead to someone not being considered for a job interview, for example.

13.4 ENGLISH AMONG THE LANGUAGES OF THE WORLD

Another advantage of being a linguist is the view it gives you on to your own language, from an outside perspective. As a native speaker of German, I had the advantage of learning English at school and reflecting on the language in a different way from most native speakers of English. I only started to gain an understanding of German when I learnt other languages, realizing that structures I had taken for granted could be expressed in very different ways in other languages.

It can be a big eye-opener to learn that your language differs from others, and to understand how such differences arise, where they are likely to be found and to what extremes they can diverge from the language you know. We could think of it as a picture of Earth from space, something that captures people's imagination, looking in on something familiar from the outside.

We can learn that English is special in a number of ways, for example in grammar. Take the verbal inflections discussed in chapter 5. While many languages have an unmarked form in the third person singular, this is the only form in English that receives additional marking by -*s*.

13.5 PRACTICAL OUTCOMES

There are many other practical issues where knowledge of linguistics can be useful and help your personal development. For example, you may want to learn a new language. You could reflect on different approaches to language learning, choosing the style that is most appropriate for you. You could ensure that factors affecting language learning are right for you, such as having access to speakers, being highly motivated and developing a get-go attitude about not being shy when using the second language, albeit 'incorrectly' at first.

13.6 THE BIG QUESTION: WHEN WILL I KNOW IT ALL?

Starting to learn about a field of study like linguistics, you may wonder when you will know it all; or, at least, when you will know enough to understand the subject. If you have a look at those who are ahead of you in their studies, graduates, lecturers, textbook authors and even famous linguists, it may seem a daunting task. Yet, all those people had to start from the beginning as well. Also, I very much doubt that any of those people (even the famous linguists) 'know it all'. Rather, they know where to go if they have a question. They read a lot, if they have the time, go to conferences and talk to other linguists. They are in constant pursuit of knowledge, which is what research really is about.

The point is: we do not know it all yet – but rather we are trying to figure it out. The more you read and engage with the topic, the more you will find out and the more you will understand. At all times, it is a good idea not to be afraid to say that you do not know about something. Since nobody can know it all – and if they say they do they are probably lying – there is no reason to be ashamed of not knowing something. The person you ask about the topic in question may not know the answer, either, and you could set out to find out about the topic together. Or they know the answer, and will be able to help you in your quest to understand more about the topic.

I have always found it easier to learn from others by asking simple questions than by hiding the fact that I do not know something. Engaging with others, being curious about linguistics and following your interests will motivate you to learn more. And you will see: soon you will know much more than others who are starting out, and you will feel comfortable to discuss what you have learnt with others. And when the situation arises where you do not understand a specific issue, you can always ask – most of us do!

FURTHER READING

For different speech styles and different attitudes to language see, for example, Meyerhoff (2011) *Introducing sociolinguistics*. Aitchison (2012) *Language change: progress or decay?* is also a highly accessible book on a similar topic.

If you are interesting in how English spelling developed, see Crystal (2013) *Spell it out: the singular story of English spelling*. David Crystal has written many highly accessible books about language worth exploring, if you want to find out more. For example, his book about the 'decline' of the English language because of texting, Crystal (2009) *txtng the gr8 db8*.

References

Aitchison, Jean (2012) *Language change: progress or decay?* 4th edition. Cambridge University Press.

Allan, Keith (2010) *The western classical tradition in linguistics.* 2nd edition. Equinox.

Ashby, Patricia (2011) *Understanding phonetics.* Routledge.

Atkins, Sue and Michael Rundell (2008) *The Oxford guide to practical lexicography.* Oxford University Press.

Austin, Peter and Julia Sallabank (2011, eds.) *The Cambridge handbook of endangered languages.* Cambridge University Press.

Baugh, Albert C. and Thomas Cable (2012) *A history of the English language.* 6th edition. Routledge.

Birner, Betty (2012) *Introduction to pragmatics.* Wiley-Blackwell.

Brown, Leah and Matthew Dryer (2008) 'The verbs for "and" in Walman, a Torricelli language of Papua New Guinea', *Language* 84, 3: 528–565.

Cruse, Alan (2011) *Meaning in language.* 3rd edition. Oxford University Press.

Crystal, David (2009) *txtng the gr8 db8.* Oxford University Press.

——(2013) *Spell it out: the singular story of English spelling.* Profile Books.

Cutting, Joan (2007) *Pragmatics and discourse.* 2nd edition. Routledge.

Davenport, Mike and S.J. Hannahs (2010) *Introducing phonetics and phonology.* 3rd edition. Routledge.

Doherty-Sneddon, Gwyneth (2008) 'The great baby signing debate: academia meets public interest', *The Psychologist* 21(4): 300–303.

Dörnyei, Zoltan (2007) *Research methods in applied linguistics.* Oxford University Press.

Dryer, Matthew S. and Martin Haspelmath (eds.) (2013) *The world atlas of language structures online.* Leipzig: Max Planck Institute for Evolutionary Anthropology. (Available online at www.wals.info [accessed 4.8.2014]

Evans, Nicholas (2000) 'Iwaidjan, a very un-Australian language family', *Linguistic Typology* 4(1): 91–142.

——(2010) *Dying words: endangered languages and what they have to tell us.* Wiley-Blackwell.

Everett, Daniel (2005) 'Cultural constraints on grammar and cognition in Pirahã', *Current Anthropology* 46(4): 621–646.

——(2009) *Don't sleep, there are snakes.* Profile Books.

Fitch, W. Tecumseh (2010) *The evolution of language.* Cambridge University Press.

Gardner-Chloros, Penelope (2009) *Code-switching.* Cambridge University Press.

Gil, David (2013) 'Riau Indonesian: a language without nouns and verbs', in Jan Rijkhoff and Eva van Lier (eds.) *Flexible word classes: typological studies of underspecified parts of speech.* Oxford University Press, pp. 89–130.

Greetham, Bryan (2013) *How to write better essays.* 3rd edition. Palgrave.

Gries, Stefan (2013) *Statistics for linguistics with R.* Mouton de Gruyter.

Gussenhoven, Carlos and Haike Jacobs (2011) *Understanding phonology.* 3rd edition. Routledge.

Halliday, M.A.K. and Colin Yallop (2007) *Lexicology: a short introduction.* Continuum.

Harrison, K. David (2010) *The last speakers: the quest to save the world's most endangered languages.* National Geographic Society.

Haspelmath, Martin and Andrea Sims (2010) *Understanding morphology.* Routledge.

Hauser, Mark D., Noam Chomsky and W. Tecumseh Fitch (2002) 'The faculty of language: what is it, who has it, and how did it evolve?', *Science* 298, 1569–1579.

Hurford, James A. (2014) *Language origins: a slim guide.* Oxford University Press.

Jones, Rodney (2012) *Discourse analysis: a resource book for students.* Routledge.

Kendon, Adam (2004) *Gesture: visible action as utterance.* Cambridge University Press.

Knight, Rachael-Anne (2012) *Phonetics: a coursebook.* Cambridge University Press.

Kuhn, Thomas S. (1962) *The structure of scientific revolutions.* University of Chicago Press.

Lewis, M. Paul, Gary F. Simons, and Charles D. Fennig (2014, eds.) *Ethnologue: languages of the world*, 17th edition. Dallas, Texas: SIL International. Online version: www.ethnologue. com.

Lieber, Rochelle (2010) *Introducing morphology.* Cambridge University Press.

Litosseliti, Lia (2010, ed.) *Research methods in linguistics.* Continuum.

Löbner, Sebastian (2013) *Understanding semantics.* Routledge.

Macaulay, Monica A. (2006) *Surviving linguistics: a guide for graduate students.* Cascadilla Press.

Malmkjaer, Kirsten (2013, ed.) *The Routledge linguistics encyclopedia.* 3rd edition. Routledge.

Matthews, Peter H. (2014) *The concise Oxford dictionary of linguistics.* Oxford University Press.

McGregor, William (2009) *Linguistics: an introduction.* Continuum.

McNeill, David (2012) *How language began: gesture and speech in human evolution.* Cambridge University Press.

Meyerhoff, Miriam (2011) *Introducing sociolinguistics.* 2nd edition. Routledge.

Moravcsik, Edith A. (2012) *Introducing language typology.* Cambridge University Press.

Murray, Neil (2012) *Writing essays in English language and linguistics: principles, tips and strategies for undergraduates.* Cambridge University Press.

Paltridge, Brian (2012) *Discourse analysis.* Continuum.

Pereltsvaig, Asya (2012) *The languages of the world: an introduction.* Cambridge University Press.

Podesva, Robert J. and Devyani Sharma (2013, eds.) *Research methods in linguistics.* Cambridge University Press.

Pope, Rob (2012) *Studying English literature and language.* Routledge.

Rijkhoff, Jan and Eva van Lier (2013, eds.) *Flexible word classes: typological studies of underspecified parts of speech.* Oxford University Press.

Ringe, Don and Joseph S. Eska (2013) *Historical linguistics: toward a twenty-first century reintegration.* Cambridge University Press.

Rook, Steve (2013) *The graduate career guidebook.* Palgrave.

Sakel, Jeanette (1999) 'Passive in Greenlandic'. Unpublished MA thesis, University of Aarhus, Denmark.

Sakel, Jeanette and Daniel Everett (2012) *Linguistic fieldwork: a student guide.* Cambridge University Press.

Schachter, Paul and Timothy Shopen (2007) 'Parts of speech systems', in Timothy Shopen (ed.) *Language typology and syntactic description, 1: Clause structure.* 2nd edition. Cambridge University Press, pp. 1–60.

Sealey, Alison (2010) *Researching English language: a resource book for students.* Routledge.

Senft, Gunter (2014) *Understanding pragmatics.* Routledge.

Sutton-Spence, Rachel and Bencie Woll (1999) *The linguistics of British sign language: an introduction.* Cambridge University Press.

Tallerman, Maggie (2005, ed.) *Language origins: perspective on evolution.* Oxford University Press.

——(2014) *Understanding syntax.* 4th edition. Routledge.

Tomasello, Michael (2010) *Origins of human communication.* MIT Press.

Treffers-Daller, Jeanine and Jeanette Sakel (2010) *Wider perspectives and more options for English language and linguistics students.* The Higher Education Academy (HEA).

Velupillai, Viveka (2012) *An introduction to linguistic typology.* Benjamins.

Warburton, Nigel (2007) *The basics of essay writing.* Routledge.

Wodak, Ruth and Michael Meyer (2009, eds.) *Methods for critical discourse analysis.* 2nd edition. Sage.

Wray, Alison and Aileen Bloomer (2012) *Projects in linguistics and language studies.* 3rd edition. Routledge.

Yule, George (2014) *The study of language.* 5th edition. Cambridge University Press.

Glossary

abstract noun
A *noun* that denotes an abstract notion, such as *love* or *grammar*.

accusative case
A *case* that marks the *direct object*. In English object *pronouns* such as *him* and *me* appear in the accusative case, while *nouns* are not marked for *case*.

acronym
An abbreviation – often of the first letters of the meaningful words – such as *NATO* (from *North Atlantic Treaty Organization*). Often pronounced as one word (and referred to as 'initialism' when each letter is pronounced separately, such as *CD*).

action verb
A *verb* that expresses an action (such as *he walks*) rather than an *event* (such as *the book fell*).

active (voice)
The *unmarked* voice. This is the standard form and it differs from e.g. the *passive* in English.

adjective →
attributive,
predicative
A class of words that typically describe attributes of nouns, for example *beautiful*. Adjectives can be divided up into *attributive* and *predicative adjectives*, depending on their function (where they appear). Attributive adjectives appear in a *noun phrase* and modify the noun they appear with. Predicate adjectives appear in the *predicate* of a clause, for example after the *copular verb to be*.

adverb
A class of words that typically describe attributes of *verbs* or *adjectives*, such as *well*, *slowly* and *incredibly*. Adverbs typically refer to the time, place or manner in which *actions* or *events* take place, and include elements such as *tomorrow* and *soon*.

adverbial
A place within a *clause* or *sentence* which can be filled by individual words, *phrases* or *clauses*. Adverbials give more information about the *verb*, typically referring to time, place or manner in which *actions* or *events* take place. This can be done by *adverbs* such as *soon*, by *phrases* such as *in a polite way* or through *subordinate clauses*, referred to as adverbial clauses, such as *when she saw him there*. Such subordinate clauses are usually introduced by *subordinating conjunctions* such as *while*, *when*, *because*, *since* and *in order to*.

affix	A *morpheme* which is attached to another morpheme to form a word. Affix is the generic term (*hypernym*) for *suffix* (an affix that is added to the end of a word, such as *walk-ed*), *prefix* (an affix that is added to the beginning of a word, such as ***un**-able*) or *infix* (an element that appears in the middle of a word).
agent	Refers to a person (or living being) carrying out an *action*, such as the **bold** elements in the following examples: ***He** saw me. I was seen **by him**.* Agents are often, but not always, the *subjects* of *clauses* (but notice cases such as *I was seen by him* where the subject is not an agent).
agreement	The link between different elements, for example in a clause, showing grammatical features. For example *The mans eats.* In this case, the *–s* in *eats* agrees with the subject in person (a third person) and number (singular). Other types of agreement include noun phrases such as ***these** stones* (as opposed to *this stone*). In the plural, the demonstrative pronoun *these* agrees in number with the plural noun *stones*.
allophone	Variation within a *phoneme*, such as differences in pronunciation that do not lead to a difference in meaning. For example, the way the /a/ in *Manchester* is pronounced by someone from the North of England varies from the pronunciation of speakers from the South. Nonetheless, the meaning of *Manchester* is not changed.
alveolar ridge	The ridge on the upper part of the mouth, behind the teeth.
analysis	The close investigation of a set of data, for example by comparing features.
anaphora	Anaphora expresses links across the context, for example by using a *personal pronoun* to refer to a person previously introduced.
animacy	Certain grammatical structures differ depending on the animacy of the elements present. Sometimes there is a distinction between animate (*a dog*) and inanimate (*a book*).
anthropological linguistics	An area of linguistics studying the relationships between language and culture, as well as and how these are linked with thought.
antonymy	Antonyms have opposite meanings, such as *big* and *small*.
appendix	The additional information presented at the end of an essay or a book. We could say that this glossary appears in the appendix of the book. The appendix usually holds information that is relevant to the topic under discussion, but that does not form part of the core text. Things typically appearing in an appendix are the data on which a study is based, consent forms and similar information.

applied linguistics	The study of linguistics relating to real-world issues, such as the study of second language acquisition, discourse strategies or sociolinguistics. Sometimes applied linguistics is considered the opposite of *theoretical linguistics*.
arbitrary	Random, not predictable.
aspect	A grammatical category of verbs, which marks for the (internal) structure of an action or event. For example the *progressive aspect* marks for an ongoing action. The *perfect aspect* marks for an action that has finished.
auxiliary verb	An auxiliary verb such as *be, have, do* is used together with a main verb to express some grammatical categories, such as *aspect*. The *progressive aspect* he is walking is expressed by combining the main verb *walk* with the auxiliary verb *be* (in inflected form). Additionally, *walk* appears in the *present participle* form with the *–ing* ending. The combination of all of these points leads to the reading 'progressive aspect', i.e. the auxiliary as part of that construction.
baby signing	A way in which very young babies can express themselves long before they are physically able to utter their first words.
basic word order	The main word order in a language, which has the most basic (and straightforward) meaning. The basic word order of English is *SVO* (subject–verb–object), as in *he eats cake*. Other orders may be possible, but are used in very specific situations, such as *cake, he eats* (OSV) and are referred to as *marked word orders*.
behaviourism	An approach to language (including philosophy and psychology, alongside other areas of investigation) that was strong in the early twentieth century, viewing linguistic behaviour as a set of habits.
bilingualism	The ability to speak two or more languages (in the latter case this is sometimes referred to as multilingualism).
bottom-up	A study that starts by looking at the *data* and only later draws conclusions that arise from the data investigated in the study.
borrow	See 'borrowing'.
borrowing	Borrowing refers to taking over words (or other features such as grammar) from other languages. Loanwords are instances of such borrowing.
bound morpheme	A morpheme that has to appear together with another morpheme (and that cannot appear on its own). An example is *un-* in *un-able*.

by-phrase	By-phrases are a typical features of *passive clauses* and refer to the agent of an action, for example *the cake was eaten **by him***.
C	Abbreviation used for 'consonant'.
calque	A calque is a remodelling of words or elements in one language due to the influence of another. For example the English word *skyscraper* exists as a calque in German: *Wolkenkratzer* (*Wolken* = clouds, *kratzer* = scraper). In this case the structure of the English element was copied using German words.
case	Case is a grammatical category that marks for an element's function in a clause. In English, case only appears with *pronouns*. The *nominative case* is used with *subject* pronouns such as *I*, while the *accusative case* is used with *object* pronouns such as *him*.
clause	A clause is an entity of language. It contains one *predicate*. Clauses can be combined to form *complex sentences*.
closed word classes	Word classes like *pronouns* or *prepositions* for which there are a fixed number of elements. While not impossible, it is usually difficult to add new elements to a closed word class (as opposed to open word classes).
code-switching	The use of two or more languages in the same conversation.
coherence	A text is coherent if it is meaningful and logical in its context.
cohesion	A notion that refers to linguistics devices in texts that link different parts of the text, such as *anaphoric* elements used to refer back to an element introduced previously.
comparative	A grade in *adjective* and *adverb* comparison, for example *bigger* for the adjective *big*.
comparison	A way of grading adjective and adverbs in comparison to other elements in the context, for example *nice, nicer* and *nicest*, in which case *nicer* is in the *comparative* and *nicest* in the *superlative* grade.
complement clause	A *subordinate clause* that fulfils the role of *subject* or *object* within the main clause, such as *he thought **that she would stay***, in which case *that she would stay* is a subordinate clause that functions as the object of the main clause *he thought* _____ (something).
complex sentence	A sentence containing more than one *clause*, in which case the clauses could be *coordinated* or *subordinated*.
compound	The combination of two separate entities (words) into a new element, such as *greenhouse*, which is a compound of *green* and *house*.

concrete noun	A noun that refers to an entity that can be perceived by our senses, such as *house, man, fire* and *air*. It contrasts with *abstract nouns*.
conditional	A *mood* that expresses that something may happen under certain conditions.
conjunction	A word (or combination of words) that is used to link *clauses* or other elements. *Coordinating* conjunctions can coordinate two equal clauses or elements of equal weight. In English they take the forms *and, or, but*. There are many more *subordinating* conjunctions in the language, introducing clauses at a lower (subordinate) level. These include *while, because, since, in order to, so that*, and so on.
consonant	A speech sound (in contast to 'vowel').
consonant cluster	More than one consonant appearing together within the same *syllable*, such as /str/ in *straw*.
constituent	This term is often used for a *phrase* that plays a role at clause level. For example, subject, verb and object are treated as constituents.
constituent order	The order of constituents within a *clause*, often referred to as word order (yet it is not so much the order of words but the order of the phrases that makes up the constituents). The basic constituent order of English is *SVO* (subject–verb–object).
conversion	Forming a word from another word without any changes to the original form – but through changing the word class. For example *to walk → a walk* (conversion from verb to noun).
coordinating conjunction	A conjunction used to combine two elements of equal weighting. *And, or, but* in English. A coordinating conjunction can combine individual words, as in *a black **and** green car* (where *and* combines the adjectives *black* and *green*); it can combine *phrases*, such as *who do you mean, the tall lady **or** the man with the fancy hat* (where *or* combines the noun phrases *the tall lady* and *the man with the fancy hat*); or it can combine *clauses*, as in *I was going to go to bed early **but** my favourite programme started on the television* (where *but* combines the two clauses of equal weight).
coordination	The combination of two elements of equal weight, often, but not always, through the help of a coordinating *conjunction*.
copular verb	A verb that expresses an 'equals' (=) relationship, sometimes called 'linking verb'. In English, the verb *be* is the most typical copular verb (but beware: *be* can also function as a *temporal-aspectual auxiliary*). Other copular verbs include *seem, appear* and *look*, for example *you look tired*.

corpus	A collection of language *data* that is organized into a large, searchable archive.
count noun	A noun that can be counted as an individual entity, such as *a chair* or *two dogs*, as opposed to *mass nouns* that are not countable, such as *porridge*. We could, possibly, say *a porridge*, referring to one portion of porridge. Yet, in general *porridge* appears without an article *a* or *the*, while count nouns like *house* or *cat* have to appear with an article in the singular. Thus, we can say *porridge is nice*, while **cat is nice* does not work (it would have to be *the cat is nice* instead).
cross-linguistic	Across a range of different languages.
CV	Curriculum Vitae. This is usually adjusted to the purpose you are using it for (i.e. targeting a specific employer), listing your qualifications and skills relating to a specific role; or a generic CV used to collect the different achievements you have made.
data	Language material – be it recordings of spoken language, *texts*, or similar. When you analyse something, you can refer to that as your data.
dative case	A *case* that exists in a number of European languages (such as German) to mark a *recipient* (such as *er gab **mir** das Buch*, 'he gave me the book', where *me* appears in the dative case). The dative also appears after a number of *prepositions* that require this case in German.
declarative	Used for a *clause* or *sentence* that makes a statement, as opposed to other sentence types such as orders (*imperative*) or questions (*interrogative*).
declension	A term traditionally used for the *inflection* of *nouns* and words classes other than verbs.
definite article	An article that is usually used with a known entity. The English definite article is *the*.
deictic centre	The place that serves as the *here*, *now*, and *I* of deictic expressions, i.e. the centre of reference of what is said.
deixis	Elements that are linked to the context in which they are used, including person deixis such as *I* (which depends on who is speaking), place deixis such as *there* (which is relative to the context in which it is used), and time deixis such as *now*.
demonstrative pronoun	A pronoun that is used to point to things. In English these are *this*, *that*, *these* and *those*. Demonstrative pronouns can relate to something 'near', such as *this* and something further away, such as *that*.
dental	A sound produced at the position of the teeth, such as [t].

dependent	An element in a *phrase* that is not the *head*, i.e. the other elements of phrases. In the noun phrase **the big** house, *house* is the head and *the* and *big* are hence the dependents.
derivation	A process through which new words can be formed. In most cases, derivation is carried out through the addition of *affixes*, yet there are also instances such as *conversion* where no morphological elements are added.
descriptive (grammar)	An approach to language and grammar that looks at what people do and say, rather than expecting (or prescribing) speakers to act in a certain way.
determiner	A term used for a specific position in a *noun phrase*. Typically, elements such as articles act as determiners in noun phrases, such as **the** house, where *the* is the determiner.
dialect	A variety of language spoken in a certain geographical and/ or social or other environment.
diphthong	A combination of two *vowels* (or a vowel and a so-called 'semi-vowel') to make a new sound.
direct object	This element is often just referred to as the object of a clause. We speak of the direct object when wanting to distinguish it from the indirect object of *ditransitive clauses*.
discourse	This is the cover-term for all language in use, whether spoken, written or signed. Discourse can involve various speakers/writers/signers or just one person using language.
discourse marker	A word or combination of words that is used to structure the discourse. This includes hesitation markers such as *uh*, which would not generally be written down, but also tag questions like *isn't it?* that would appear in *informal* writing.
discussion	In essay writing: the part of the essay where the findings are discussed in the light of the literature set out in the *literature review*. Ask yourself if your data show something new, or whether they confirm what others have found before you. This part of the essay is often the most important part as it draws together the different strands on which an essay is based. A good discussion that uses critical reflection is the first step towards a good mark.
ditransitive verb	A verb that appears with three underlying *noun phrases*, such as *give*, which requires an *agent* (who carries out the giving, e.g. *a child*), a *patient* (the thing that is given, e.g. *a book*) and a *recipient* (the one receiving the thing that is given, e.g. *me*)

domain	In *sociolinguistics*: a situation, setting or people with whom you use language in a specific way. For example, *bilinguals* may use different languages in different domains: in the home domain they use German, while in the work domain they use English.
edited volume	Typically a book or issue of a journal that one or more academics in the field have put together, usually about a specific topic.
ethics	The morals of research: for example by making sure that our research does not harm the people we investigate.
event	A term sometimes used to describe the *semantics* of *verbs*: verbs that do not denote *actions*, for example *fall* and *sleep*.
feminine	A grammatical *gender* form, often loosely based on sex.
filler	In discourse: a *discourse marker* that fills a gap, for example when the speaker needs more time to think, for example *well* in the following context: *And then, well, I walked over to her.*
finite	Used for verbs that are *inflected*. This means they mark for *tense*, and they may agree with the subject (and/or object) in *person*, *number* or *gender*. In English it is usually the first verb in linear order within a *verb phrase* that is finite, such as *could* and *was* in *I **could** have eaten something earlier, but **wasn't** hungry.* Contrasts with infinitive verbs.
forensic linguistics	A subfield of linguistics that uses linguistic tools to investigate language use in a legal context. Most prominently, forensic linguistics can help to establish evidence of crimes (e.g. what are the characteristics of the person who said that, could this letter have been written by the same person, and so on).
formal	As a register, formal is the language use that is more guarded, often more traditional. It is usually found in official written documentation and formal situations of spoken language. It contrasts with *informal* language use.
free morpheme	A morpheme that can appear on its own (as a word), such as *able* in the example *un-able*. It contrasts with *bound morphemes*.
fricative	A continuous sound that is produced by air passing through a restricted cavity, leading to friction. For example [s] and [f] are fricatives.
fusion	In *morphology* the situation where one *morpheme* combines different meanings and functions. For example, *–s* appearing in English verbs (e.g. *he walk-**s***) is a fused morpheme containing the functions third *person*, *singular* and *present tense*.

future tense	A way to mark the verb to express that an *action* or *event* is to happen in the future.
gender	In grammar, this is a way to divide nouns into different groupings, for example *masculine*, *feminine* and *neuter*. Gender becomes evident through agreement, such as by articles or adjectives in a noun phrase. Sometimes these systems are based on other distinctions than sex and are also referred to as *class*.
genitive	A *case* in a number of European languages that expresses possessions and association. The English *–'s* in *this guy's clothes* could be referred to as a 'genitive marker'.
genitive pronoun	A pronoun indicating a relationship of 'belonging', such as *his, yours, my, our, their*. Some linguists use the term *possessive pronoun* interchangeably.
gloss	The word-by-word translation and grammatical information often given in linguistic examples of other languages. The gloss is usually the line directly below the data, followed by an overall translation in the third line of the example.
glottal stop	A sound that is produced by obstructing the airflow at the glottis (at the back of the throat), written [ʔ] in IPA and sometimes represented by an apostrophe in writing. It appears in examples such as *oh ' oh*.
grammar	The underlying structures used to put words together to make sense of words. All languages have grammar, whether there is a *written* grammatical description of that language or not. Grammar can be viewed *prescriptively*, as in 'you have to adhere to the rules of grammar', or *descriptively*, as in 'what do speakers actually do when speaking their language?'. The latter is the perspective taken by most linguists.
habitual	A way to mark the verb to express that an action happens habitually. In English, the use of the *present tense* without further marking usually expresses such a meaning. For example *he walks* may be understood as 'he walks as a habit', whereas an ongoing action in the present tense would be expressed using the progressive aspects, as in *he is walking*.
head	The main elements in a phrase. Thus, the head of a *noun phrase* is a *noun*.
homograph	Words that are written in the same way but have different meanings (and even different pronunciations), such as *object* in *an **object*** (with the stress on the /o/) and *I **object** to your behaviour* (with the stress on the /e/).

homonym	Words that are written and pronounced in the same way but that have different meanings, such as *can* (as in the modal verb *I* **can** *do something*) and *can* (as in a **can**, a tin).
homophone	Words that sound the same, but that may be written in different ways, such as *it's* and *its* in English.
hypernym	The cover term for a number of words (hyponyms), such as *flower* (as the hypernym) for *daisy, buttercup, poppy*. These hyponyms can also be hypernyms, for example *buttercup* as the hypernym for sub-categories such as *meadow buttercup, bulbous buttercup, creeping buttercup*.
hyponym	A sub-category of a hypernym, such as *buzzard* (hyponym) as a sub-category of the hypernym *bird of prey*.
hypothesis	In a research study: the expectation you have as to what the outcome of your study may be. The hypothesis is then tested in the study to see to which degree this expectation can be confirmed (or not).
imperative	A form of <u>*verbs*</u> (cf. <u>*mood*</u>) used to express an order. In English, subjects of imperatives are left out, such as *walk!* where the subject is understood as the addressee 'you'.
inceptive	A way to mark a verb in some languages to express that an action is beginning, such as *he starts to read*.
indefinite article	An article that appears with nouns that are not <u>*definite*</u> in the context, for example because they have not been talked about before. In English the indefinite article is *a* (with the variation *an* in certain contexts), as in *I have bought* **a** *car*.
indicative	The most basic mood form of a verb, which contrasts with e.g. *imperative*. Thus, when a verb is in its most basic, unmarked mood, it is said to be in the indicative. For example *you walk* is in the indicative, while *walk!* is in the imperative.
indirect object	An object that appears with <u>*distransitive*</u> verbs, usually marking the recipient, as in *I gave* **her** *the book*. In some languages the indirect object receives a specific case marker, such as the <u>*dative case*</u> in German.
inference	Drawing conclusions about issues on the basis of available information.
infinitive	A form of the verb that exists in some languages (such as English); it is a non-finite verb form and appears in some forms of subordinations, or as the citation form of a verb. In English it appears with the infinitive marker *to*, e.g. *to walk*.

infix	An *affix* that appears in the middle of a word (e.g. in the middle of a root). Some English swearwords make use of infixation, such as *abso-freakin'-lutely*, where the infix *freakin'* appears in the middle of the word (the root) *absolute*, which cannot normally be split up further.
inflection	The grammatical marking of *verbs*, *nouns* and other word classes by certain categories (such as *person*, *gender*, *number*, *case*).
informal	In terms of the register used: a less guarded way of speaking and writing.
interrogative clause	A clause that expresses a *question*, including 'content questions' like *Who is she?* and 'yes/no questions' such as *Are you sure this is right?*
interrogative pronoun	A *pronoun* – also referred to as *wh-word* in English used to introduce content questions, such as *who, where, which, why, when, what* and *how*.
intransitive verb	A verb that appears with only a subject – such as *I **walk***.
introduction	In an essay: the first section of the essay that introduces the topic. It tends to present the main research question or hypothesis, and gives an overview of the essay.
inversion	In English: the switching of place of *subject* and *auxiliary* verb, for example in yes–no *questions* and in *negated* clauses.
involuntary action	In the *semantics* of *verbs*: an action that happens without anybody acting consciously.
IPA	The International Phonetics Alphabet, a way of representing sounds consistently across all languages in the world.
irregular	In grammar: a structure that does not follow the normal patterns. For example irregular *plural* forms other than the *regular –s/-es*.
iterative	A verbal *aspect* that expresses the repetition of an action, such as to clap repeatedly.
journal article	An academic essay that is published in a journal. Such journals are often specialized in specific areas of study (such as *International Journal of American Linguistics* which specializes in the indigenous languages of the Americas, publishing articles about this subject).
labial	A sound produced at the lips.
language acquisition	The learning of language. This covers first language acquisition (abbreviated to L1) and second (and subsequent) language acquisition (L2, L3, etc.).
language change	The way a language changes over time, either through sound changes or other internal mechanisms, or through *contact* with other languages.

language contact	Language contact happens when two or more languages are spoken alongside one another, often by *bilingual* speakers. Language contact can lead to changes in one or more of the languages, such as through borrowing.
language teaching	Instruction in a language, typically in a classroom setting.
larynx	Area at the back of the throat where the *vocal cords* are located.
lateral	A consonant produced by the air being blocked from the centre, while escaping at each side of the tongue.
lexeme	The linguistic term for *word*.
Lexical Functional Grammar	An approach to grammar that has its roots in generative grammar, a formal way of analysing language.
lexicon	In terms of the mental lexicon: the words a speaker knows in a language. These can include words that are actively produced (spoken), as well as those only known passively.
linguistic typology	An area of linguistics which looks at the similarities and differences between the languages of the world.
literal	In terms of meaning: the plain, direct reading of a *text*, i.e. its literal meaning.
literature review	The part of an essay where you discuss what others have written about the topic (or related topics), critically reflecting on how certain approaches differ.
loanword	A word that originates in another language, such as *igloo*, which is a loanword from Inuit (Greenlandic). The pronunciation, spelling, meaning and function of such loanwords can differ from that in the original language. For example, *igloo* (written *igdlo*, *illu*) means 'house' in Greenlandic and does not refer to a house made of ice.
logic	An approach to reasoning, common in the studies of philosophy and mathematics. Some linguists also investigate the logic of linguistic expression.
main clause	In a complex sentence: the clause that contains the main *verb*.
marked	In relation to grammar, marked refers to something that is not the default. A marked plural, for example, is a form that has no –*s* (or –*es*). For example *ox – oxen* displays a marked *plural*.
marked word order	A word order that deviates from the basic word order of a language. In English, this would refer to any other order than *SVO*.

masculine	A grammatical *gender*. In English, gender is only distinguished in singular personal pronouns, where *he* is the masculine form. In other languages (such as Spanish), gender appears in many other areas of grammar.
mass noun	A type of noun that refers to an overall entity, rather than separable (individual) pieces. In this way, mass nouns do not appear with the quantifier *many*, e.g. **many porridges*. Instead, we could use the quantifier *a lot of* or we would have to specify the container used for the mass noun, e.g. *many bowls of porridge*. Some mass nouns can be used as *count nouns* as well under certain circumstances, e.g. *many waters* could be used to refer to many lakes.
metaphor	A figure of speech: an equation of something with something else that is otherwise unrelated in its *literal* meaning. A *broken heart*, for example, is not broken in reality, but it may feel this way to the person experiencing this feeling, using a metaphor to express this.
metaphorical	In the sense of a *metaphor*.
method	A way in which a study is carried out, such as how data are collected and analysed.
metonymy	A figure of speech similar to *metaphor*, yet where a concept is expressed through a related meaning (as opposed to an entirely unrelated meaning in metaphors).
Middle English	The varieties of English that developed following the Norman invasion (in 1066), and that were spoken (and written) until the late fifteenth century.
minimalism	An approach to grammar that has its roots in the 'generative approach' to language. A highly formalized way to analyse language structures, in particular *syntax*.
mixed methods study	A study that makes use of both *qualitative* and *quantitative* methods.
modal auxiliary	An *auxiliary verb* that expresses *mood*. In English, the main modal auxiliaries are *should, could, ought, would, might, may, can, will, must* and *shall*.
modality	A way to express wishes, beliefs, attitudes and obligations to what is said. This could be done through *modal auxiliaries*, or through certain *complex sentences*, e.g. *It is important that he read the letter immediately.* [note also the additional use of the *subjunctive* with *read*]

Modern English	The English spoken since the late fifteenth century, after the completion of the so-called 'Great Vowel Shift'. There are various forms of Modern English (such as the 'Early Modern English' of Shakespeare, which some may argue is quite different from the Modern English spoken today).
modifier	An element that is added to describe or classify another element. For example, an *adjective* can act as a modifier for a *noun*, as in **good** work. In this case, *good* tells us more about *work*. Similarly, in *straight into the house*, *straight* modifies the *preposition into*.
mood	Verbal inflection expressing distinctions between *indicative*, *subjunctive* and *imperative* in some languages. Related to – and sometimes used synonymously with – 'mode'.
morpheme	Often defined as the smallest meaningful unit. An element of meaning from which words are built up. Either *free* (appearing on its own as a *word*) or *bound* (always appearing with one or more other morphemes).
morphology	The study of how words are built up, looking at how new words are formed, as well as how existing words can be modified in different grammatical environments.
motherese	The language spoken by mothers to their children, which often has a higher pitch than regular language. Also known by its formal term 'child directed speech'.
multilingualism	The situation where individuals or societies use more than one language in everyday life. Often used synonymously with *bilingualism*.
nasal	Referring to the nose, e.g. when relating to *nasal consonants*.
nasal consonant	A consonant that is pronounced by part of the airflow going through the nasal cavity.
negation	A grammatical structure that adds a negative meaning to the clause, for example through the addition of a negation marker *no*.
networking	Getting to know other people in the field, engaging with them professionally. Networking can happen at employment fairs (by talking to possible employers), through engagement with student societies, the student union or similar.
neuter	A grammatical *gender* (see also *masculine* and *feminine*).
nominative case	A grammatical *case*. The nominative case is the *unmarked* case. In languages that have nominative–*accusative* case marking, it marks the *subjects* of *clauses*.
non-finite	A verb that is not *inflected*, for example a *present participle*, *past participle* or *infinitive* form.

non-literal	The meaning conveyed is not the direct, literal reading. This is the case, for example, in *metaphors*.
noun	A word class that refers to a concept, such as a thing or an abstract entity. There are different kinds of nouns depending on their semantics (*concrete noun*, *abstract noun*) or the grammatical environment in which they occur (*mass noun*, *count noun*). Nouns referring to names (of people, places, institutions, products and the like) are usually called *proper nouns*.
noun class	In some languages nouns can be divided up into different classes, depending on the grammatical contexts in which they occur and/or the meaning of the nouns. Class is often discussed in combination with *gender*, and some linguists argue that the two should be treated under the same heading.
noun phrase	A noun or pronoun appearing on its own or with immediate companions, such as definite articles, adjectives and relative clauses. The following examples are all noun phrases: *he*, *the girl*, *the big car*, *a very different story*. Also the following is one noun phrase in which the *relative clause* functions as a *modifier*: *A single occurrence **that changed my approach to this subject***.
number	The grammatical category of marking for *singular* and *plural*. Some languages also have further numbers, such as a *dual*.
numeral	The *word class* of numerals contains what we call 'number' in plain English, i.e. elements like *one*, *two*, *three* and so on.
object	A grammatical function in a clause, for example *cake* in: *I like **cake***. *Transitive* verbs appear with (or at least have underlying) objects. *Ditransitive verbs* even have two underlying objects, as in *I brought **him cake***. Where *him* and *cake* are two separate objects in the clause.
object noun phrase	A noun phrase that has the function of *object* in a clause.
observer's paradox	When recording language *data*: the fact that speakers alter their language when they see a microphone, camera, or have a linguist observer present in the situation. Hence, the language recorded during such a session may be very different from the language used once the microphone is switched off.
Old English	The variety of English from the onset of Anglo-Saxon settlement in the British Isles to the Norman invasion in 1066.
onomatopoeic	An expression is onomatopoeic when the sound used in language models the actual sound, such as *cuckoo*, which mimics the call of this bird.

open word class	A word class to which new elements can be added without difficulties, in particular the classes *nouns*, *verbs* and *adjectives*.
operationalization	In a research study and essay: making clear how you are going to classify the data, including how you are going to measure the features you are interested in. You are expected to give a clear overview of this prior to (presenting) your research.
oral consonant	A consonant that is pronounced by air passing through the oral cavity (when the air does not access the *nasal* cavity).
paradigm	A way to organise linguistic information into a table or present such information consistently. For example, *verb inflection* can be presented in a paradigm to show the different forms for *person*, *number*, *gender* or other categories.
participant observation	In a research study to observe and keep diary notes without conducting *experiments* or *recording* language data.
participle	A *non-finite* form of the verb, used to form certain *tense*, *aspect* or *voice* structures. Includes the *present participle* and the *past participle*. Participles can be used to e.g. form the *progressive aspect*: *he **was walking***. The combination of the present participle *walking* with an auxiliary (*was*) forms the progressive aspect.
particle	A term that is sometimes used for *closed class words* that are not classified as belonging to other word classes, sometimes also used for *discourse markers*.
parts of speech	Another term for *word classes*. An *adjective* is a part of speech.
passive voice	A *voice* structure of English where emphasis is taken away from the *agent* and focus is on what happened to the *patient*.
past participle	A *non-finite* verb form that is used in certain constructions to express *aspectual* and *temporal* distinctions, as well as *voice*. For example *he has **eaten**, it was **arranged** (by me)*.
past tense	A type of verb *inflection* that marks that an *action* or *event* took place in the past.
patient	A semantic role that refers to an entity undergoing an action or event, such as *the cake* in *I ate **the cake***.
peer-review	A process through which others of equal status or a similar background (your 'peers') read and comment on your work. For example anonymous peer-review of journal articles, which is common practice.
perfect	An *aspect* that marks that an *action* or *event* has been completed.

person	In linguistics: refers to the difference between *I* (first person), *you* (second person) and *he/she/it* (third person), which may play a role in a language's *inflection* system.
personal pronoun	A word class that contains elements that can replace full noun phrases, for example **he** (*the man*) or **it** (*the new car*). It refers not just to 'persons' as such, despite the name.
personal skills	A term used in this book to refer to the skills you acquire that are not necessarily directly linked to any employment or subject knowledge, but that may contribute to your personal development.
phoneme	An entity of sound in a language that distinguishes meaning. For example, *card* and *hard* are different words. The sounds that distinguish the meaning are /c/ and /h/, which are hence phonemes of English.
phonetics	The study of sound, in particular how sounds are produced and the acoustic qualities of sounds.
phonology	The study of sound systems in specific languages, for example how *phonemes* are arrange in individual languages.
phrase	A term used to refer to elements that are linked together, forming one *constituent*, such as the *noun phrase* in the house or the *verb phrase* will be eaten.
pilot study	A small 'test' study carried out prior to a big research study in order to see if the *methods* work and whether there are other aspects to consider (which may not always be possible once a big study has started).
plagiarism	Presenting others' words, ideas or thoughts as your own, without quoting the original source. For example copying parts of essays from others and presenting these as your own work. Plagiarism is usually investigated and often punished.
plosive	A consonant sound that is produced in such a way that the airflow is fully restricted and then released in one 'explosion', such as /p/ or /t/.
pluperfect	A *perfect aspect* in the *past tense*: something that has been completed in the past, for example. *He **had eaten** dinner (when I came to visit).*
plural	A grammatical number referring to *two* or more.
polysemy	A word is polysemous if it has various different meanings.
possessive pronoun	A pronoun indicating a relationship of 'belonging', such as *his, yours, my, our, their.* Some linguists use the term *genitive pronoun* interchangeably.
pragmatics	The study of meaning in context, different from *semantics* (lexical meaning). Pragmatics looks at the way in which utterances are understood in context.

predicate	In a *sentence*: the part of the sentence that contains the *verb* as well as other elements such as an *object*.
predicative adjective	An adjective used in the *predicate* of a *clause*, for example after a *copular verb*: *he is **tall***, where *tall* is a predicatively used adjective. This differs from *attributive* (or modifying) adjectives that appear within a *noun phrase* (such as *the **tall** man*).
prefix	An *affix* that is added before a base (i.e. a word), for example *un-* in ***un**-available*. It contrasts with *suffix*, which appears after a base.
preposition	A *closed word class* of items that generally express the location in time or space of something in relation to something else. Examples from English include *in, at, around* and *with*.
prescriptive (grammar)	An approach to grammar that takes grammar books and written-down rules of grammar as the main indicator for how to speak correctly.
present participle	A *non-finite* verb form that is used in certain constructions to express *aspectual* and *temporal* distinctions. For example in *he is **walking***, the *progressive aspect* is formed by the auxiliary verb *be* and the present participle ending *walking* in *–ing*.
present tense	A type of verb *inflection* that marks that an *action* or *event* takes place at the time of speaking (or the time taken as the 'now').
presupposition	An assumption that can be arrived at by the information given.
preterite	A term used for the *past tense* (and corresponding to the past tense in English) that is used in a range of readings in different grammatical traditions (including past events completed in the past and similar). It is hence often avoided by linguists talking about *tense* and *aspect*.
progressive	An aspect that is ongoing, such as *he is walking*, where the progressive aspect is formed by combining the *temporal-aspectual auxiliary is* with the *present participle walking*.
pronoun	A *closed word class* consisting of elements that can, in some cases, replace other elements in a clause. Subcategories include *personal pronouns, interrogative pronouns* and *demonstrative pronouns*.
proper noun	A name. A noun that refers to a person, place, product, institution or otherwise specific individual entity.
proposition	In language: the main part of an expression.

psycholinguistics	An area within the study of linguistics concerned with language and cognition. For example, psycholinguistics investigates how language is produced or comprehended.
punctual	An *aspect*, expressing that an action happens only once. For example a sneeze can be described as a punctual action.
qualitative study	A study in which one or few participants' language use is investigated in closer detail, for example by recording a long segment of language use and investigating specific features therein.
quantifier	A word class that expresses quantity, such as *many, few, all*.
quantitative study	A study in which many participants are compared across one, or a range of, features. This could be done, for example, by asking many speakers the same question, or by repeating a linguistic experiment with a range of speakers.
question	A type of clause that is uttered to elicit an answer from the person spoken to. Also referred to as *interrogative clause*.
reading group	A group of students getting together each week to discuss the tasks set that week, for example reading they had to do on the course.
reference	A book, article or other piece of academic work mentioned in e.g. an essay, often in the following format (Sakel 2015; this would be the way you would reference the current book). Make sure the references in your text are repeated in your list of references at the end of the essay, and that only references in that list appear throughout the text.
reflexive pronoun	A *pronoun* that is used to refer back to another element in the *clause*, for example when *subject* and *object* of a clause refer to the same person: *he is critically evaluating **himself** in the mirror.*
regular	For example in *paradigms* when the structures encountered are as expected without exception. The opposite of *irregular*.
relative clause	A *clause* that can act as a *modifier* in a *noun phrase*, telling us more about the *head noun*, such as *the students **who had done their homework** achieved high marks.* Relative clauses can be restrictive (as in the example), limiting the reading of the noun, or non-restrictive, making a generic statement about the noun.
research impact	The outcomes of research being applicable and useable within society. For example, research into language teaching is highly impactful if it shows that a certain approach is advantageous, and if that approach is subsequently taken up by others as a result of the original research.

research monograph	A book written by one (or a few) individual author(s) outlining a piece of research.
research question	A question or *hypothesis* posed at the beginning of a study (for example in an essay), which is then tested in the subsequent research.
research report	A report highlighting the findings of a piece of research. Depending on the audience, the report may be written for the general public, or it could be aimed at a certain group of readers with specific background knowledge. Reports may be shorter than traditional essays and may not include a detailed review of the literature.
results	In an essay: the section where the results of a study are presented, prior to their discussion and interpretation of the data.
rhetoric	The art of speaking, and of convincing others through speech.
Role and Reference Grammar	A formal approach to grammar that originates in functional and *typological* approaches.
second language acquisition	The study of how a second language is acquired, looking for example, at the factors that lead to success in language learning, the paths that learners take in acquiring a second language or how a first language can influence a second language during acquisition.
semantic role	The role a noun phrase plays in a clause, for example the *agent* carrying out an action or a *recipient* receiving something.
semantics	The study of meaning, including lexical meaning.
sentence	A *syntactic* construct, sometimes used synonymously with *clause*, yet the term 'sentence' is often used to refer to a combination of clauses.
sign language	Languages used by deaf communities, making use of gestures and other signs that are not based on sound. There are also sign languages aimed at hearing communities, for example 'Makaton', a sign language developed for use with disabled people and the so-called 'baby signing' developed to enable very young babies to communicate.
significant	In statistics: the results indicate that there is a correlation between the elements investigated, i.e. that it is likely that something happened because of something else, rather than being due to chance.
singular	A grammatical *number* referring to *one*.

sociolinguistics	A wide area of linguistics concerned with the study of language in use, for example in looking at varieties ('dialects' or 'sociolects') of a language, investigating how interactions take place or studying *bilingualism*.
special edition	In publications: an edition of a journal that is edited by one or more 'guest editors' and that contains articles about a specific subject explored in that edition.
split infinitive	In English: the situation where an element appears between the infinitive marker *to* and the verb form, for example *to proudly present*, in which case *proudly* 'splits' the two elements of the infinitive.
state	In *verb semantics* a situation where no action takes place, such as *the book is lying on the table*.
statistics	A way to calculate the probability of something, for example whether a certain outcome is likely to be for a certain cause.
structure	A general term referring to elements of grammar.
subject	In the clause: the noun phrase that generally attracts the main focus. The only noun phrase of an intransitive verb such as *sleep*, as in **she** *sleeps*, in which case *she* is the subject.
subject benchmark statement	In the UK, a list of subjects expected to be treated and skills expected to be developed in individual subject areas.
subject noun phrase	A noun phrase that appears in the position of the subject in a clause.
subjunctive	A *mood* that is typical of some languages (such as Spanish), where it appears in certain types of *subordinate clauses*. It only exists in very formal varieties of English and does not take special inflection forms. For example: *I expect that he **read** this*, in which case *read* is in the subjunctive and appears in the *unmarked* morphological form of the verb, as opposed to the *marked* form *reads*, which may have been expected in this place instead.
subordinate clause	A clause that is part of a *complex sentence* and which appears at a lower level than the *main clause*.
subordinating conjunction	A conjunction (a word class) that is used to introduce subordinate clauses, such as *because*, *while*, and *that* (+ a clause).
subordination	The process by which *clauses* are combined in such a way that one clause is the main clause and others are subordinated. This means they appear as part of the main clause (for example as *subject* or *object*) in the case of *complement clauses*, in an *adverbial* position in the case of *adverbial clauses* or, for example, as part of a *noun phrase* in the case of *relative clauses*.

suffix	An *affix* that is added at the end of a 'base', i.e. that appears at the end of a word, such as *–ed* in *watch-ed*. Because it is added to something at the end, the dash – indicating where it is attached to the other word – appears before it.
superlative	In adjective (and adverb) comparison, the highest level, such as *best, clearest, nastiest* and the like.
SVO	The abbreviation for *subject, verb* and *object*. The *unmarked word order* of English.
syllable	A unit of sound that is divided on its sound-related features (its structure, its rhythm) rather than its meaning. Syllable structures can vary across languages; they are given as CVC or CVC(C) or similar, with C referring to *consonant* and V referring to *vowel*.
syncretism	Overlap between some categories, such as in a *paradigm*. In English, there is syncretism in the verbal paradigm in that *I* **walk** and *they* **walk** (as well as all other forms other than the third person singular) are the same.
synonym	A word with the same meaning.
syntax	The study of sentence structures.
tag question	A short question, often at the end of a statement of the type *isn't it?, is it? right?* or the like. This short tag may serve to elicit a response from the person spoken to, or it may merely be used as a discourse marker in the context.
teaching materials	Exercises and other materials (such as texts, collections from books, etc.) used for teaching purposes.
temporal-aspectual auxiliary	An auxiliary that is used to mark tense or aspect. In English, there are two such auxiliaries: *have* and *be*.
tense	A grammatical way of marking when an action takes place in relation to a point in time 'now', typically the *past*, the *present* or the *future*.
TESOL	Teachers of English to Speakers of Other Languages.
text	A continuous piece of language data, which can be spoken, written or signed.
textspeak	A term often used for abbreviations and other innovations used in text messages and other digital communication.
theoretical linguistics	A broadly defined area of linguistics that deals with language as an abstract concept, often contrasted with *applied linguistics*.
theory	An established, usually tested approach to a subject.
third person singular	Elements in the singular that do not refer to *I* or *you*, i.e. noun phrases that can be replaced by *he, she, it*.
top-down	An approach to a topic where you think about your *hypothesis* first before looking at any actual *data*.

transcription	Writing down language data that have been recorded (audio or video).
transferable skill	A skill that can be used in contexts other than where it was originally acquired. For example, the skills to write essays can be used in composing other texts.
transitive verb	A verb that appears with two *noun phrases*: the *subject* and an *object*.
transitivity	A concept relating to *verbs*, differentiating between *intransitive verbs* that appear with a *subject*, *transitive verbs* that appear with a subject and an *object*, and sometimes also *ditransitive verbs* that appear with a subject and two objects.
translation	Transferring a text from one language to another. Simultaneous translation of spoken language is usually referred to as 'interpretation'.
triangulation	Looking at a phenomenon from a range of different perspectives, such as by combining a *qualitative* research study with a *quantitative study*.
trill	A sound which is 'rolled', such as the rolled /r/, which can be produced at the tip of the tongue (as in Spanish) or at the back of the throat (typical of some varieties of French and German).
turn-taking	In a conversation the change of who is speaking.
unmarked	A structure in its basic, default form. The opposite of *marked*.
uvula	A small protrusion at the back of the throat where uvular sounds are produced.
V	Abbreviation used for 'vowel'.
velum	The soft palate at the back of the mouth.
verb	A word class that typically expresses *actions* and *events*. Often divided up by their grammatical context, such as *intransitive verbs* and *transitive verbs*.
verb class	Some languages have verb classes, which may present differences in the way the verbs are *inflected*. For example Spanish verbs can be divided up into different classes depending on whether the infinitive forms of the verbs end in *-ar, -er* or *-ir*.
verb phrase	A term used in this book to refer to the elements that make up a *verb*. This includes auxiliaries and similar elements, such as *would have left* would be classified as a verb phrase. This term is sometimes avoided because of the theoretical implications in some areas of grammar.
vocabulary	Words. For example the words you know in a language.

vocal cords	Membranes in the larynx, at the base of the throat, through which air passes on its way to the mouth/nose. The position of the vocal cords determines whether the sounds produced are *voiced* or *voiceless*.
voice	In grammar: the way in which an action can be viewed and expressed in a different way. For example by changing the *subject* and/or *object* of the clause. In English this is done by the *passive* voice, which takes the focus away from the person acting, e.g. *The pizza has already been eaten (by me – if you need to know).*
voiced	A sound produced with the *vocal cords* almost closed, leading them to vibrate and producing a voiced sound.
voiceless	A sound that is pronounced with the *vocal cords* wide open, leading to an unvoiced or voiceless sound.
vowel	A type of sound, such as [a], [e] or [o], represented in the *IPA* in a *vowel triangle*.
vowel triangle	A schematic representation of vowel sounds in the *IPA*.
wh-word	A word used to form questions (among some other functions). In English most of these words begin in *wh–*, which is how this term came about. They include: *which*, *where*, *what* and the exception *how*.
word	An entity of language, generally an item that appears on its own. Linguists prefer the term *lexeme*.
word class	A category that a word belongs to, such as *noun*, *verb*, *adjective*, *preposition*. Also referred to as *part of speech*.
word order	The order of words (or, more precisely *phrases* – i.e. *constituents*) in a clause, therefore often called *constituent order*. In English, the *unmarked word order* is *SVO* (i.e. *subject*, *verb*, *object*).

Index of languages

Classical Greek 81
Danish 10, 18
Finnish 10, 11, 31, 32, 116
French 1, 3, 26, 54, 74, 102, 110, 157
German 1, 11, 26, 36, 45, 51, 64, 129, 130, 138, 140, 142, 144, 157
Greek 50, 82
Greenlandic 87, 98, 146
Hindi 81
Igbo 44
Italian 3, 110
Iwaidja 44
Japanese 30
Latin 3, 50, 81, 82, 83, 110, 130
Mandarin Chinese 60

Middle English 19, 147
Modern English 19, 128, 148
Mosetén 10, 11, 42, 59, 81, 82
Norwegian 18
Old English 19, 128, 149
Old French 82
Pirahã 16, 22, 78, 79, 80, 84
Portuguese 3, 52, 62, 110
Riau Indonesian 44
Romanian 3, 110
Sanskrit 81
Spanish 3, 10, 18, 54, 56, 58, 60, 85, 89, 90, 95, 110, 147, 155, 157
Swedish 18, 31, 116
Walman 44

Index

abstract noun 33, 37, 38, 135
accusative case 64, 70, 135
acronym 33, 45, 135
action verb 38, 135
active (voice) 67, 68, 135
adjective 33, 35, 41, 42, 43, 44, 45, 46, 48, 49, 50, 52, 53, 57, 59, 62, 63, 64, 65, 66, 68, 69, 70, 82, 135
adverb 33, 38, 41, 63, 64, 66, 73, 83, 135
adverbial 68, 69, 135
affix 46, 47, 48, 49, 59, 136
agent 65, 67, 136
agreement 46, 52, 53, 57, 58, 64, 136
allophone 31, 136
alveolar ridge 27, 29, 136
analysis 2, 9, 41, 47, 59, 76, 77, 80, 86, 93, 94, 95, 97, 102, 103, 120, 136
anaphora 76, 136
animacy 52, 136
anthropological linguistics 1, 136
antonymy 71, 73, 136
appendix 102, 103, 136
applied linguistics 2, 81, 84, 98, 137, 156
arbitrary 10, 11, 137
aspect 40, 46, 50, 53, 54, 55, 56, 60, 137, 139, 143, 145, 150, 151, 152, 153, 156
attributive 135, 152
auxiliary verb 40, 53, 55, 56, 57, 67, 70, 137

baby signing 10, 15, 21, 22, 137, 154
basic word order 61, 137, 146
behaviourism 81, 137
bilingual 3, 85, 89, 90, 94, 95, 101, 111, 113, 116, 137, 142, 146, 148, 155

bilingualism 95, 111, 113, 116, 137, 148, 155
bottom-up 80, 137
borrow 35, 50, 137
borrowing 137, 146
bound morpheme 47, 48, 59, 137, 142
by-phrase 68, 138

calque 129, 138
case 46, 50, 51, 64, 138
clause 3, 57, 61, 62, 63, 64, 65, 66, 67, 68, 135, 136, 138, 139, 140, 141, 145, 146, 148, 149, 152, 153, 154, 155, 158
closed word class 35, 36, 44, 138, 150, 152
code-switching 94, 95, 98, 138
coherence 75, 76, 129, 138
cohesion 75, 76, 129, 138
comparative 53, 138
comparison 48, 50, 52, 53, 138, 156
complement clause 68, 69, 138, 155
complex sentence 3, 61, 68, 138, 146, 147, 155
compound 34, 46, 97, 138
concrete noun 36, 37, 45, 139, 149
conditional 56, 139
conjunction 43, 44, 68, 135, 139, 155
consonant 23, 25, 27, 28, 29, 31, 32, 138, 139, 146, 148, 150, 151, 156
consonant cluster 31, 32, 139
constituent 63, 139, 151, 158
constituent order 63, 139, 158
conversion 38, 49, 139, 141
coordinating conjunction 43, 68, 139
coordination 68, 139
copular verb 41, 57, 65, 66, 67, 70, 135, 139, 152

corpus 86, 93, 94, 97, 140
count noun 42, 140, 147, 149
cross-linguistics 3, 140
CV 117, 124, 125, 126, 140

data 5, 7, 15, 31, 32, 78, 79, 80, 81, 83, 85,
    86, 87, 90, 91, 92, 93, 94, 95, 96, 97, 98,
    100, 103, 120, 136, 137, 140, 141, 147,
    149, 150, 154, 156, 157
dative case 64, 140, 144
declarative 66, 67, 140
declension 50, 140
definite article 37, 38, 42, 46, 48, 52, 57,
    62, 64, 140, 144, 149
deictic centre 75, 140
deixis 75, 140
demonstrative pronoun 42, 52, 63, 136,
    140, 152
dental 27, 29, 30, 42, 50, 74, 102, 140
dependent (grammar) 70, 141
derivation 46, 48, 49, 59, 141
descriptive (grammar) 10, 20, 78, 81, 82,
    129, 141, 143
determiner 52, 63, 64, 70, 141
dialect 2, 18, 24, 30, 41, 86, 96, 109, 110,
    127, 129, 141, 155
diphthong 27, 31, 32, 141
direct object 61, 62, 64, 135, 141, 144
discourse 2, 12, 21, 71, 75, 76, 77, 78, 98,
    115, 119, 127, 129, 137, 141, 142, 150,
    156,
discourse marker 13, 43, 76, 129, 141,
    142, 150, 156
discussion (essay) 102, 103, 104, 141, 154
ditransitive verb 39, 40, 45, 64, 141, 149,
    157
domain 90, 142

edited volume 44, 111, 112, 115, 142, 155
ethics 85, 91, 96, 97, 142
event 35, 38, 40, 54, 55, 56, 65, 135, 137,
    142, 143, 150, 152, 157

feminine 51, 52, 58, 59, 60, 142, 143, 148
filler 11, 13, 35, 43, 129, 142

finite 70, 144, 150, 152
forensic linguistics 2, 70, 142
formal 11, 13, 14, 17, 20, 21, 33, 50, 128,
    129, 130, 142, 155
free morpheme 47, 59, 142
fricative 28, 29, 30, 142
fusion 59, 142
future tense 54, 55, 56, 75, 83, 143,
    156

gender 46, 50, 51, 52, 53, 57, 93, 142, 143,
    145, 147, 148, 149, 150
genitive 82, 143, 151
genitive pronoun 143, 151
gloss 52, 87, 143
glottal stop 59, 143
grammar 1, 2, 3, 4, 9, 11, 13, 14, 20, 21,
    22, 36, 38, 43, 44, 46, 47, 49, 50, 51, 53,
    61, 66, 71, 74, 78, 81, 82, 83, 92, 116,
    127, 130, 143

habitual 55, 143
head 63, 64, 70, 141, 143, 153
homograph 73, 143
homonym 71, 73, 143
homophone 73, 144
hypernym 73, 136, 144
hyponym 71, 73, 144
hypothesis 79, 80, 84, 102, 144, 145, 154,
    156

imperative 56, 60, 140, 144, 148
inceptive 55, 144
indefinite article 37, 42, 62, 144
indicative 56, 60, 144, 148
indirect object 64, 141, 144
inference 71, 73, 74, 76, 144
infinitive 38, 54, 56, 70, 82, 83, 126, 130,
    142, 144, 148, 155, 157
infix 46, 47, 59, 136, 145
inflection 44, 46, 48, 49, 50, 51, 53, 54, 55,
    56, 57, 81, 130, 140, 145, 148, 150, 151,
    152, 155
informal 13, 17, 20, 67, 111, 128, 129, 139,
    141, 142, 145

interrogative clause 66, 67, 140, 145, 153
interrogative pronoun 42, 66, 145, 152
intransitive verb 39, 40, 64, 65, 145, 155, 157
introduction (essay) 102, 103, 105, 113, 145
inversion 56, 66, 67, 70, 145
involuntary action 38, 145
IPA 23, 24, 25, 26, 28, 29, 30, 32, 143, 145, 158
irregular 50, 53, 54, 88, 145, 153
iterative 55, 59, 145

journal article 98, 101, 102, 109, 111, 112, 113, 114, 145, 150

labial 27, 30, 145
language acquisition 1, 2, 9, 81, 98, 102, 111, 137, 145, 154
language change 1, 2, 20, 73, 81, 84, 131, 145
language contact 1, 3, 111, 128, 146
language teaching 2, 146, 153
larynx 27, 146, 158
lateral 28, 146
lexeme 59, 146, 158
Lexical Functional Grammar 1, 81, 146
lexicon 35, 146
linguistic typology 1, 2, 3, 44, 59, 70, 146
literal 71, 72, 146, 147, 149
literature review 94, 97, 102, 103, 104, 114, 146
loanword 31, 36, 50, 116, 137, 146,
logic 73, 74, 76, 77, 138, 146

main clause 68, 138, 146, 155
marked 50, 51, 52, 53, 55, 56, 57, 59, 64, 67, 83, 130, 135, 144, 146, 148, 155, 157
marked word order 61, 137, 146, 156, 158
masculine 51, 52, 64, 143, 147, 148
mass noun 42, 140, 147, 149
metaphor 71, 72, 73, 147, 149
metaphorical 72, 73, 147

method 83, 84, 85, 86, 87, 88, 89, 90, 91, 93, 94, 95, 97, 98, 102, 103, 104, 111, 113, 147, 151
metonymy 71, 72, 147
Middle English 19, 147
minimalism 81, 147
mixed methods study 89, 98, 147
modal auxiliary 40, 56, 57, 147
modality 50, 53, 55, 56, 147
Modern English 19, 128, 148
modifier 52, 63, 64, 68, 69, 70, 148, 149, 153
mood 40, 46, 50, 53, 54, 55, 56, 139, 144, 147, 148, 155
morpheme 46, 47, 48, 52, 53, 59, 87, 136, 137, 142, 148
morphology 1, 4, 44, 46, 59, 142, 148
motherese 11, 148
multilingualism 1, 2, 137, 148

nasal 27, 28, 29, 30, 148, 150
nasal consonant 27, 148
negation 17, 61, 66, 67, 74, 102, 148
networking 8, 99, 100, 114, 120, 123, 148
neuter 51, 143, 148
nominative case 64, 70, 138, 148
non-finite 70, 144, 148, 150, 152
non-literal 71, 72, 149
noun 2, 3, 16, 33, 35, 36, 37, 38, 39, 40, 43, 44, 45, 46, 48, 49, 50, 51, 52, 53, 57, 58, 62, 63, 64, 65, 67, 68, 69, 70, 135, 136, 139, 140, 143, 143, 145, 147, 148, 149, 150, 152, 158
noun class 52, 149
noun phrase 35, 39, 41, 42, 43, 45, 52, 58, 62, 63, 64, 65, 68, 69, 135, 136, 139, 141, 143, 149, 151, 152, 153, 154, 155, 156, 157
number (grammar) 46, 50, 51, 52, 53, 57, 58, 59, 136, 142, 145, 149150, 154
numeral 63, 78, 149

object 45, 52, 59, 60, 61, 62, 63, 64, 65, 66, 67, 68, 70, 135, 137, 138, 139, 141, 142,

143, 144, 149, 152, 153, 155, 156, 157, 158
object noun phrase 62, 64, 149
observer's paradox 90, 91, 96, 149
Old English 19, 128, 149
onomatopoeic 11, 149
open word class 35, 36, 138, 150
operationalization 94, 150
oral consonant 27, 150

paradigm (in grammar) 51, 53, 57, 58, 60, 150, 153, 156
paradigm (in scientific study) 81, 83
participant observation 92, 150
participle 53, 54, 55, 137, 148, 150, 152
particle 42, 43, 150
part of speech 35, 150, 158
passive voice 67, 68, 135, 138, 146, 150, 158
past participle 53, 54, 55, 148, 150
past tense 49, 53, 54, 55, 56, 57, 58, 60, 85, 88, 89, 150, 151, 152
patient 65, 67, 68, 141, 150
peer-review 101, 112, 113, 116, 150
perfect 54, 55, 56, 137, 150, 151
person 46, 47, 48, 49, 50, 51, 53, 56, 57, 58, 59, 60, 70, 75, 136, 140, 142, 145, 150, 151, 156
personal pronoun 42, 51, 56, 58, 60, 64, 75, 76, 136, 147, 151, 152
personal skills 4, 151
phoneme 23, 30, 32, 136, 151
phonetics 1, 4, 23, 24, 32, 145, 151
phonology 1, 4, 23, 31, 32, 47, 151
phrase 35, 37, 39, 40, 41, 42, 43, 45, 52, 56, 58, 61, 62, 63, 64, 65, 66, 68, 69, 70, 78, 88, 135, 136, 138, 139, 141, 142, 143, 149, 151, 152, 153, 154, 155, 156, 157, 158
pilot study 89, 94, 151
plagiarism 102, 108, 116, 151
plosive 28, 29, 151
pluperfect 55, 151
plural 38, 42, 46, 47, 48, 49, 50, 51, 52, 57, 58, 59, 60, 70, 136, 145, 146, 149, 151

polysemy 71, 72, 73, 151
possessive pronoun 42, 63, 143, 151
pragmatics 1, 4, 71, 74, 77, 151
predicate 61, 66, 68, 69, 70, 77, 135, 138, 152
predicative adjective 70, 135, 152
prefix 46, 47, 136, 152
preposition 3, 7, 35, 36, 42, 44, 45, 62, 66, 73, 81, 82, 138, 140, 148, 152, 158
prescriptive (grammar) 10, 20, 82, 83, 130, 143, 152
present participle 53, 55, 137, 148, 150, 152
present tense 49, 53, 54, 55, 56, 57, 58, 70, 142, 143, 152
presupposition 71, 74, 152
preterite 55, 152
progressive 54, 55, 56, 137, 143, 150, 152
pronoun 2, 17, 19, 23, 24, 25, 26, 26, 27, 28, 29, 30, 31, 32, 33, 42, 50, 51, 52, 56, 58, 60, 63, 64, 66, 72, 75, 76, 109, 110, 112, 135, 136, 138, 140, 143, 144, 145, 147, 148, 149, 150, 151, 152, 153, 158
proper noun 45, 149, 152
proposition 71, 74, 76, 77, 84, 152
psycholinguistics 1, 2, 9, 93, 153
punctual 55, 153

qualitative study 88, 89, 90, 91, 92, 93, 94, 98, 147, 153, 157
quantifier 43, 147, 153
quantitative study 88, 89 90, 92, 93, 94, 95, 98, 147, 153, 157
question (grammar) 17, 42, 43, 56, 61, 66, 67, 140, 141, 145, 153, 156, 158

reading group 99, 100, 153
reference (literature) 5, 86, 97, 99, 101, 102, 103, 104, 105, 110, 112, 113, 114, 153
reflexive pronoun 42, 153
regular (grammar) 50, 53, 54, 88, 145, 153
relative clause 68, 69, 149, 153, 155
research impact 97, 153

research monograph 111, 112, 115, 154
research question 85, 86, 88, 89, 90, 102, 103, 105, 111, 113, 145, 154
research report 111, 154
results 80, 83, 85, 88, 93, 95, 97, 100, 101, 102, 103, 104, 106, 113, 116, 154
rhetoric 12, 154
Role and Reference Grammar 1, 81, 154

second language acquisition 2, 102, 137, 154
semantic role 61, 65, 150, 154
semantics 1, 4, 38, 71, 74, 77, 142, 145, 149, 151, 154, 155
sentence 3, 4, 35, 61, 63, 65, 66, 67, 68, 69, 70, 71, 74, 75, 76, 87, 138, 140, 146, 147, 152, 154, 155, 156
sign language 9, 10, 14, 15, 21, 154
significant 95, 154
singular 42, 48, 49, 50, 51, 52, 53, 56, 57, 58, 59, 64, 70, 87, 130, 136, 140, 142, 147, 149, 154, 156
sociolinguistics 1, 2, 84, 89, 131, 137, 142, 155
special edition 111, 155
split infinitive 82, 83, 126, 130, 155
state 38, 41, 49, 155
statistics 88, 93, 95, 98, 154, 155
structure (of a language) 2, 3, 14, 22, 143, 155
subject 45, 48, 49, 57, 58, 59, 60, 61, 62, 63, 64, 65, 66, 67, 69, 70, 136, 137, 138, 139, 142, 144, 145, 148, 153, 155, 156, 157, 158
subject benchmark statement 3, 9, 126, 155
subject noun phrase 58, 62, 155
subjunctive 56, 60, 84, 147, 148, 155
subordinate clause 54, 68, 69, 135, 138, 155
subordinating conjunction 43, 135, 139, 155
subordination 43, 68, 69, 78, 144, 155
suffix 46, 47, 48, 49, 50, 52, 53, 56, 59, 83, 136, 152, 156

superlative 53, 138, 156
SVO 61, 62, 137, 139, 146, 156, 158
syllable 27, 30, 31, 32, 47, 139, 156
syncretism 60, 156
synonym 71, 73, 148, 156
syntax 1, 4, 69, 70, 147, 156

tag question 43, 141, 156
teaching materials 111, 156
temporal-aspectual auxiliary 40, 139, 156
tense 40, 46, 47, 49, 50, 53, 54, 55, 56, 57, 58, 59, 60, 70, 83, 85, 88, 89, 90, 96, 142, 143, 150, 151, 152, 156
TESOL 122, 156
text 75, 76, 113, 114, 115, 129, 138, 146, 156
textspeak 13, 156
theoretical linguistics 2, 78, 81, 137, 156
theory 78, 79, 80, 81, 83, 84, 105, 156
third person singular 48, 49, 51, 53, 56, 57, 79, 130, 142, 156
top-down 80, 156
transcription 32, 91, 157
transferable skill 4, 118, 119, 120, 157
transitive verb 33, 39, 45, 64, 65, 149, 157
transitivity 39, 43, 44, 157
translation 19, 20, 22, 52, 71, 87, 143, 157
triangulation 89, 157
trill 28, 157
turn-taking 76, 157

unmarked 53, 56, 59, 130, 135, 144, 148, 155, 156, 157, 158
uvula 27, 157

velum 27, 157
verb 2, 16, 33, 35, 36, 38, 39, 40, 41, 42, 43, 44, 45, 46, 48, 49, 50, 53, 54, 55, 56, 57, 58, 59, 60, 61, 62, 63, 64, 65, 66, 67, 68, 69, 70, 72, 82, 83, 130, 135, 137, 139, 141, 142, 143, 144, 145, 146, 147, 148, 149, 150, 152, 155, 157
verb class 54, 157

verb phrase 40, 45, 56, 62, 63, 64, 142,
   151, 157
vocabulary 45, 116, 129, 157
vocal cords 27, 28, 29, 146, 158
voice 61, 66, 67, 68, 135, 150, 158
voiced 28, 29, 158
voiceless 28, 29, 158
vowel 16, 23, 25, 26, 27, 29, 30, 31, 32, 139,
   141, 148, 156, 157, 158
vowel triangle 25, 26, 27, 158

wh-word 42, 145, 158
word 2, 4, 10, 11, 14, 15, 17, 18, 20, 23, 24,
   33, 34, 35, 36, 158
word class 4, 33, 35, 36, 37, 38, 39, 40, 41,
   42, 43, 44, 45, 46, 48, 49, 63, 86, 95,
   138, 139, 145, 149, 150, 151, 152, 153,
   155, 157, 158
word order 61, 63, 137, 139, 146, 156,
   158